FANTASTIC SUPERCARS

FANTASTIC SUPERCARS

RACING CARS FOR THE ROAD

Serge Bellu

12, avenue d'Italie
75013 Paris
France
Internet: www.solar.tm.fr
Series director: Renaud de Laborderie
Page design: Graph'M

This edition first published in 2004 by Haynes Publishing
Translated into English by Jon Pressnell

A catalogue record for this book is available from the British Library.

ISBN 1 84425 111 X

Library of Congress Catalog Card No. 2004104452

Haynes Publishing, Sparkford
Yeovil, Somerset BA22 7JJ, UK
Tel: 01963 443030 Fax: 01963 440001
E-mail: sales@haynes.co.uk
Web site: www.haynes.co.uk

Haynes North America Inc., 861 Lawrence Drive,
Newbury Park, California 91320, USA

Printed in Italy

FOREWORD

In the world of exceptional motor cars there is a rarefied aristocracy of truly fantastic supercars – machines that are nothing less than RACING CARS FOR THE ROAD. These are cars that have motor sport in their genes – touring cars that are closely derived from competition machines.

These cars aren't two-a-penny, and the very fact of their origins means they are sophisticated in the extreme. Their mechanicals are conceived for maximum performance, their presentation is irreproachable, their design has been arrived at without any concession or compromise, and without much thought of commercial realities.

Often these cars have ended up on the road by chance – or out of necessity. To conform to the demands of homologation, race cars frequently had to be produced in at least a small series. Then, on the other hand, there have been various cars which began life as racing prototypes pure and simple, but which ended up being converted for road use by one coachbuilder or another.

We have selected 35 of these RACING CARS FOR THE ROAD, with a preference for those which really can trace their roots back to the world of motor sport. We have thus excluded all those GTs that have been derived from regular road cars (such as the Alpine A110 Berlinette, the Porsche 356, the Chrysler Viper GTS…). By the same token we have omitted those GTs that were never really used on the open road, even if this was in theory possible (for example the Porsche 934, the Nissan R381, the Ferrari 250 GTO…).

It goes without saying that our choice hasn't been exhaustive, because these things can only be subjective. What we've tried to do, rather, is to present an array of superbly engineered and beautifully bodied cars that count among the most desirable race-bred machines in the world. These RACING CARS FOR THE ROAD truly are the most fantastic of supercars.

1927 – 1931

BUGATTI 43 GRAND SPORT

The purest of thoroughbreds

As passionate about horse-racing as about engineering, Ettore Bugatti had envisaged bridging road and track 30 years before Enzo Ferrari. His emblematic model of the 1920s, the Type 35, was to spawn countless variations, some more unlikely than others. In the beginning the Type 35 was a Grand Prix race-car, the exact equivalent of today's Formula 1 single-seaters. But in the roaring twenties spilling into either camp was possible and a certain confusion was encouraged by the legislation of the time. All you had to do was put headlamps and mudguards on a Type 35 and you had a car for a Sunday drive in the country…

Launched with a 2-litre engine, the Type 35 was available over the years in three further forms: a 35T with a 2.3-litre engine; a 35B with a supercharged 2.3-litre unit; a 35C with a blown 2-litre. Alongside this array of thoroughbreds Bugatti envisaged the creation of a true grand tourer, by taking the heart of the 35B, its supercharged straight-eight, as well as its clutch and its front and rear suspension; the front and rear axles, meanwhile, came from the Type 38. To satisfy a clientele of 'gentleman drivers', Bugatti equipped the car with a less skimpy body than that of the Type 35. That said, it remained very spartan: the sports tourer had only one door, on the left-hand side, as the spare wheel was mounted on the right-hand side. The body itself took the form of a fuselage ending in a pointed boat-tail. The eight-branch light-alloy wheels were like those of the Type 35, but surmounted by simple cycle wings.

On sale from spring 1928, the Grand Sport had its show debut at that year's Paris *salon*; the first car went to racing driver Pierre de Vizcaya. The lively open tourer soon made a name for itself in competition, winning the 1928 Monte Carlo and then the Paris-Saint-Raphaël ladies rally.

During summer 1929 Bugatti announced an evolution of the model, the Type 43A, characterised by its less rudimentary bodywork. With its rounded tail complete

TECHNICAL SPECIFICATION	
CONFIGURATION	FRONT ENGINE; RWD
STRUCTURE	SEPARATE LADDER CHASSIS
ENGINE	8-CYLINDER IN-LINE
VALVEGEAR	TWIN OVERHEAD CAMSHAFTS
CAPACITY	2,262CC (60MM X 100MM)
POWER	120BHP
FUEL SYSTEM	ZENITH/SOLEX CARBURETTOR; ROOTS SUPERCHARGER
GEARBOX	4-SPEED
WHEELBASE & TRACK	297CM; 125CM FRONT AND REAR
WEIGHT	1,250KG
TYRES	28 X 4.95
MAXIMUM SPEED	106MPH (170KPH)
NUMBER BUILT	160

IN HIS ADVERTISING SLOGANS OF THE 1920S ETTORE BUGATTI TALKED OF 'LE PUR SANG DE L'AUTOMOBILE'. SIRED BY THE LEGENDARY TYPE 35, THE TYPE 43 GRAND SPORT WELL AND TRULY DESERVED SUCH AN APPELLATION.

▲ *The second-generation Type 43, the 43A, adopted a more comfortable American-inspired style of bodywork.*

with dickey seat, and its raised moulding highlighting the waistline and surrounding the cockpit, not to mention its twin tail-mounted spares, the Type 43A had a definite American flavour. More conveniently, too, there were now doors on both sides of the body.

For more demanding customers, it was always possible, of course, to have Lavocat et Marsaud or Letourneur et Marchand confect special coachwork…

1928 ▪ 1934

MERCEDES-BENZ MODEL SSK

The German offensive

The arrival of Ferdinand Porsche at Untertürckheim ushered in a new era in the evolution of Mercedes motor cars. In July 1923 the short-tempered engineer stormed out of Austro-Daimler, the Austrian branch of Daimler Motoren-Gesellschaft where he had worked since 1905, and took the post of technical director at the mother enterprise in Germany, manufacturer of Mercedes cars.

Aged 48, Porsche succeeded Paul Daimler, Gottlieb Daimler's son, who left to work at Horch. At the same time as bringing a degree of order to the passenger-car range, Porsche occupied himself with the development of several competition models. One of these was to be a bridge between the road and the track, between a touring car and a competition car. Thanks to its multi-faceted character – its ability to shine in the rarified atmosphere of concours d'élégance as much as in the rough-and-tumble of competition – the Model S did much to create the notion of a 'Grand Touring' motor car.

In essence the Model S was based on the Model K, an imposing chassis designed to take coachwork of a certain substance. The first examples of the Model S were built in 1926, but the car's sporting career only began the following year, with a debut at the 19 June 1927 inaugural race at the Nürburgring in the Eifel mountains. To enlarge its client base, Mercedes-Benz came up with a new version intended to take more comfortable bodywork: this was the Model SS. Less low-slung than the S, it was powered by a new variant of the 7.1-litre engine, offering 170bhp in normal use and 225bhp with the supercharger engaged.

▲▶ *The SSK could either take on an out-and-out sporting look, with cycle wings (right) or else become more civilised if full-length wings and running-boards were fitted.*

THE MERCEDES-BENZ SSK IS ONE OF THE MOST ICONIC OF CARS. THIS MONUMENTAL MACHINE WAS THE CROWNING GLORY OF A FABULOUS SERIES OF MODELS BEARING THE HANDPRINT OF FERDINAND PORSCHE HIMSELF.

MERCEDES-BENZ MODEL SSK 1928 • 1934

TECHNICAL SPECIFICATION

CONFIGURATION	FRONT ENGINE; RWD
STRUCTURE	SEPARATE CHASSIS
ENGINE	6-CYLINDER IN-LINE
VALVEGEAR	OHV
CAPACITY	7,065CC (100MM X 150MM)
POWER	180BHP/250BHP AT 3,300RPM
FUEL SYSTEM	SINGLE CARBURETTOR; ROOTS SUPERCHARGER
GEARBOX	4-SPEED
WHEELBASE & TRACK	295CM; 142CM FRONT AND REAR
LENGTH/WIDTH/HEIGHT	425CM/170CM/172.5CM
WEIGHT	1,700KG
TYRES	6.50 X 20IN
MAXIMUM SPEED	118MPH (190KPH)

At the beginning of the 1930s hillclimbing was attracting good crowds in central Europe, and Mercedes-Benz was determined to play a part, to showcase the versatility of its products. But when it came to climbing the steep escarpments of the Swiss, Austrian or Bavarian Alps the S and SS seemed clumsily large. To make them better suited to mountain roads Ferdinand Porsche came up with a lighter and more compact model called the SSK, to be sold alongside the SS. Shortened by 45cm, or 17.7in (the 'K' stood for *kurz*, or 'short'), the chassis was much livelier: the monster became easier to handle in the switchbacks, and more agile around the hairpins. Mechanically, the car was more S than SS, retaining the lowered radiator and bonnet of the former model and being offered either with the 120/180bhp engine of the S or the 170/225bhp unit of the SS.

The SSK made its first appearance a few days after the SS, on 29 July 1928, at the Gabelsbach hillclimb, where it had a triumphant debut in the hands of

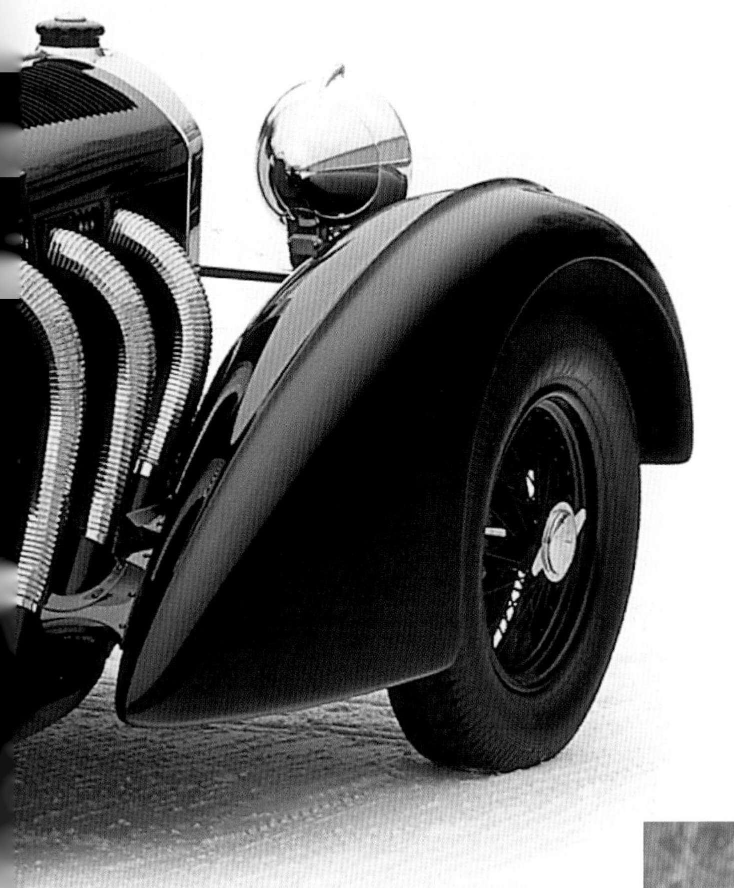

Rudolf Caracciola. In event after event the SSK forged its reputation and developed its notoreity, revealing a complex and shifting personality, capable of adapting to all situations. Just as the S before it, the SSK represented the very essence of 'grand touring', thanks to its ability to swap so easily from road to track.

Over the winter of 1928–29 only 30 or so vehicles were made, and overall production of the SSK amounted to a mere 42 cars, the last chassis being delivered to coachbuilders in 1934. Despite the eminently sporting character of the short chassis, several firms softened the car's appeal by bodying it with more refined coachwork than the austere *Sport-Zweisitzer* ('Sports Two-seater') offered by the factory. English concerns Mulliner, Corsica (chassis 36241) and Vanden Plas (chassis 36244) set to with gusto, as did Murphy in the United States and Papler and Erdmann & Rossi in Germany. Meanwhile, for Roman gentleman-driver Carlo Felice Trossi, on chassis 36038, French enterprise Saoutchik came up with the most unforgettable body of all…

In October 1928 Ferdinand Porsche bundled out of Daimler-Benz, and so it was the team led by his successor, Hans Nibel, which developed the lightweight L version of the SSK. By then, however, the Daimler-Benz board had decided to reduce its expenses and to withdraw from competition from 1931. All the same, Rudolf Caracciola kept the flag flying for the SSL, in a semi-official capacity.

▲ *Saoutchik created the body of this SSK, for racing-driver Carlo Felice Trossi.*

▶ *Only the radiator gives away the Saoutchik-bodied Trossi car as being an SSK.*

PRODUCTION FIGURES FOR THE MERCEDES-BENZ S, SS, SSK & SSKL

340cm wheelbase	*340cm wheelbase*	*295cm wheelbase*	*295cm wheelbase*
TYPE S	**TYPE SS**	**TYPE SSK**	**TYPE SSKL**
Type S (26/120/180bhp) 1926–27: 28 cars	Type SS (27/140/200bhp) 1927–28: 4 cars	Type SSK (27/170/225bhp) 1928–34: 32 cars	Type SSKL (27/240/300bhp) 1929–34: 12 cars
Type S (26/170/225bhp) 1928–30: 138 cars	Type SS (27/160/200bhp) 1928–30: 31 cars	Type SSK (26/120/180bhp) 1928–30: 10 cars	TOTAL: 12 cars
TOTAL: 166 cars	Type SS (27/170/200bhp) 1928–35: 115 cars	TOTAL: 42 cars	
	Type SS (27/180/200bhp) 1929–30: 4 cars		
	TOTAL: 154 cars		

1929 – 1930

BENTLEY 4½-LITRE SUPERCHARGED

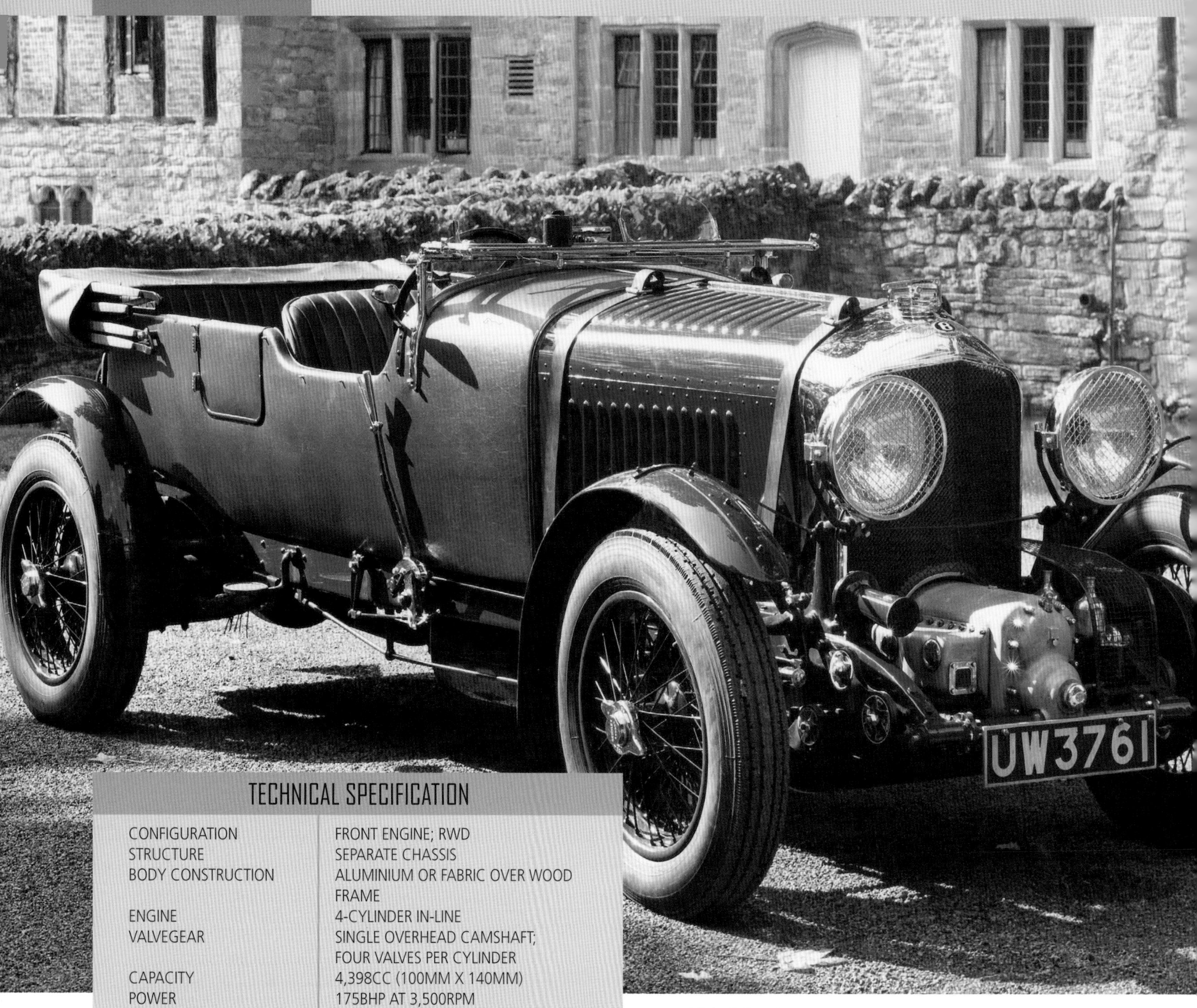

▲ *Roughly half the 'Blower Bentleys' wore Vanden Plas open tourer coachwork. This type of body was also used on the 1930 Le Mans cars. The supercharger nestling between the dumb-irons is an easy 'Blower' recognition point.*

TECHNICAL SPECIFICATION

CONFIGURATION	FRONT ENGINE; RWD
STRUCTURE	SEPARATE CHASSIS
BODY CONSTRUCTION	ALUMINIUM OR FABRIC OVER WOOD FRAME
ENGINE	4-CYLINDER IN-LINE
VALVEGEAR	SINGLE OVERHEAD CAMSHAFT; FOUR VALVES PER CYLINDER
CAPACITY	4,398CC (100MM X 140MM)
POWER	175BHP AT 3,500RPM
FUEL SYSTEM	2 SU CARBURETTORS; SUPERCHARGER
GEARBOX	4-SPEED
WHEELBASE & TRACK	330CM; 142CM FRONT AND REAR
WEIGHT	1,630KG
TYRES	6.00 X 21IN
MAXIMUM SPEED	103MPH (165KPH)
NUMBER BUILT	55 (OF WHICH 5 BIRKIN RACERS)
CHASSIS NUMBERS	HB3402 TO 3404R; HR3936 TO 3977; SM3901 TO 3925; MS3926 TO 3950

Bentley followed a faultless trajectory when it came to winning its sporting laurels, but an unfortunate dalliance with supercharging led in quick order to the company's downfall.

Fatal error

The idea behind the Le Mans 24-hours race, conceived back in 1923, was to have a contest for production cars – those, in other words, that were capable of proper road use. Right from the first race that year, the young English firm of Bentley seized the opportunity to raise its profile – the enterprise having been founded by Walter Owen Bentley in January 1919, with the 3-litre model being made from November that year.

The sole 3-litre entered in 1923 came home fourth. The following year the same team of John Duff and Frank Clement tried their luck again, and this time won the race. As a result the Bentleys acquired a reputation as being fast and reliable.

In 1925 and 1926 the French took the upper hand, with Bentley twice being beaten by the sturdy Lorraine-Dietrichs. Bentley's revenge came in 1927, with a victory for the 3-litre of Sammy Davis and John Benjafield. All the same, it was clearly time to field a more powerful machine. One of the three 1927 team cars had been a new 4½-litre model, and up until it left the track at the White House bend it certainly showed its mettle.

In 1928 Woolf Barnato and Bernard Rubin dominated the race, taking the well-honed 4½-litre across the line ahead of two hard-charging Americans, a Stutz and a Chrysler. Consecration came in 1929 with a fourth win for the 'Bentley Boys', one of the new Speed Sixes (six-cylinders and 6,597cc) leading three 4½-litres home. In 1930 the Speed Sixes confirmed their invincibility with a final one-two. Bentley was thus able to take its farewell bow, and withdraw from competition with a stunning set of laurels. Which is what happened: apart from the one-off appearances of the Embiricos streamliner in the 1949–51 races we would have to wait until the beginning of the 21st century to see Bentley return to the Sarthe… But let's go back to the 1930 race. That year, alongside the two 'works' Speed Sixes, Sir Henry Birkin (the winner in 1929) entered two cars in the name of the Honourable Miss Dorothy Paget. These were 4½-litres with the big four-cylinder engine boosted by a supercharger, at Birkin's instigation. It wasn't long before the cars became known as the 'Blower Bentleys', thanks to the massive supercharger – or 'blower' – placed in front of the radiator. WO Bentley was himself opposed to this initiative of Birkin's, saying that in his opinion it made the mechanicals less reliable. The events that ensued proved him right: both cars entered at Le Mans were forced to retire with engine problems!

To be eligible for Le Mans there had to be a run of at least 50 production 'Blowers'. Thus the factory, beginning in February 1929, made a total of 55 cars, of which 26 had open tourer coachwork by Vanden Plas, this being the body style most closely identified with Bentley's racing successes.

Despite its motor-sport laurels and the acknowledged prestige of its products, Bentley ran into unsurmountable financial difficulties which led to its absorption by Rolls-Royce in 1931. 'WO' was not slow to blame the collapse on the unfortunate supercharged 4½-litre…

1931 – 1934

ALFA ROMEO
8C 2300

The awakening of Italian style

At the end of the twenties Alfa engineer Vittorio Jano began the development of an eight-cylinder engine capable of powering both a sports car and a Grand Prix racer. The new unit was based on the six-cylinder engine used in the 6C 1750, merely with two extra cylinders being tacked on; the bore and stroke were unchanged, giving a capacity of 2.3 litres.

Throughout its life the resultant 8C 2300 evolved as a function of its dual sporting and road-car personae, in terms of its performance on one hand and its elegance on the other. Helping the process, there were three different chassis available – *Corto* (short), with a 2.75m wheelbase; *Lungo* (long), with a 3.10m wheelbase; and Monza, with an ultra-short 2.65m wheelbase.

The 8C 2300 had its debut in the 1931 Mille Miglia. This was no accident: in 1928, 1929 and 1930 Alfa Romeo had dominated the prestigious road-race with its six-cylinder models (the 6C 1500 Super Sport in the first year, and then the 1750 Gran Sport). But in 1930 the huge Mercedes-Benz SSKs had posed a real and uncompromising threat to the frail-seeming Italian machines. For that reason Alfa Romeo decided to up the ante in 1931 with the 8C 2300.

▲ *For the 1932 Villa d'Este concours d'élégance Touring created this tightly-drawn coupé called the Coupé Spyder.*

▶ *The Alfa Romeo 8C 2300 Corto in its most natural form, as a stripped-down spider by Zagato, ready for either the road or the track.*

RACING WAS ALFA ROMEO'S RAISON D'ÊTRE FOR A LONG TIME. THAT SAID, CARS SUCH AS THE 8C 2300 BRILLIANTLY MANAGED TO CULTIVATE AN AMBIGUOUS PERSONALITY, STRADDLING BOTH COMPETITION AND ROAD USE.

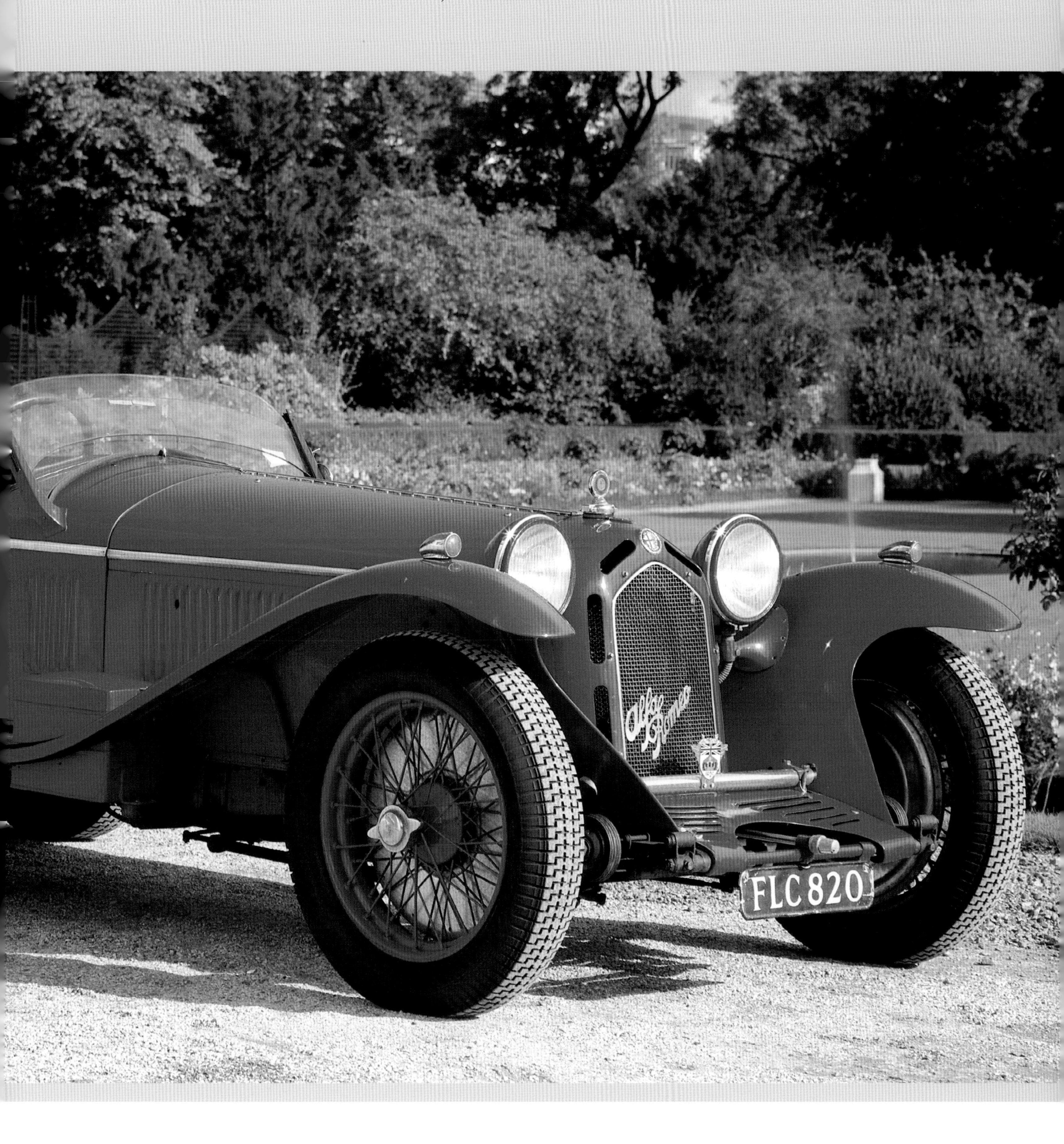

ALFA ROMEO 8C 2300 1931 • 1934

TECHNICAL SPECIFICATION

CONFIGURATION	FRONT ENGINE; RWD
STRUCTURE	SEPARATE CHASSIS
ENGINE	8-CYLINDER IN-LINE
VALVEGEAR	TWIN OVERHEAD CAMSHAFTS
CAPACITY	2,336CC (65MM X 88MM)
POWER	142BHP AT 5,000RPM
FUEL SYSTEM	CARBURETTOR/SUPERCHARGER
GEARBOX	4-SPEED
WHEELBASE & TRACK	265CM/275CM/310CM; 125CM FRONT AND REAR
WEIGHT	1,000KG
TYRES	5.50 X 19IN
MAXIMUM SPEED	106MPH (170KPH)
NUMBER BUILT	188 (OF WHICH c.50 CORTO, c.65 LUNGO, c.45 MONZA, AND c.25 UNIDENTIFIED)
CHASSIS NUMBERS	2111001 TO 2111050; 2211051 TO 2211140; 2311201 TO 2311250

But that year the Italian firm suffered from unexpected tyre problems. Arcangeli had an 'off' and it was all Nuvolari could do to stagger home in ninth place. The two 8C 2300s had to bow before the might of the impressive German machinery. Alfa Romeo would however take its revenge in 1932 and 1933, profiting from Mercedes-Benz's absence from the arena. At the same time the company shone at Le Mans, with an 8C 2300 winning the 24 Hours four times in a row – in 1931 with a long-chassis Zagato open tourer (ch 2111005); in 1932 with a short-chassis Figoni spider (ch 2111018); in 1933 with a short-chassis Zagato spider (ch 2211109); in 1934 with a short-chassis Brianza spider (ch 2311249).

The Monza didn't do too badly either. It was a dual-purpose model, taking part in either endurance rallies or Grands Prix, wearing or discarding its wings and headlamps as appropriate. It was a Monza that won the 1931 Italian GP, first time out, and a Monza that came in first in the 1934 Mille Miglia. As a parenthesis, it's worth noting that from 1933 it was the Scuderia Ferrari that was entrusted with running Alfa Romeo's competition department…

On the sidelines of this active and glorious sporting life the 8C 2300s led a sparkling 'civilian' existence far from the brouhaha of the racing circuits, in the leafy surrounds of the world of concours d'élégance. During the first year of production Zagato had the monopoly on the construction of spider coachwork. The following year rival Milan enterprise Touring took over the baton. Alongside these two-seater spiders, which despite a certain number of decorative flourishes were essentially little more than dressed-up competition cars, Touring came up with the Coupé Spyder. This small coupé, graceful and aggressive at the same time, had its debut at the September 1932 Villa d'Este concours d'élégance. Three cars were built, of which one (ch 2211053) survives.

Among other coachbuilders who took a shine to the 8C 2300 one should single out Pinin Farina and Castagna in Italy, Brandonne and Figoni in France, and Graber in Switzerland. Each in their own style sought to erase the sporting origins of the 8C 2300, and give the race-bred Alfa a sumptous set of high-society clothes.

◀ *French coachbuilder Figoni & Falaschi came up with this elegant cabriolet on the long-wheelbase chassis.*

▼ *Touring brought a few civilising touches to the 8C 2300 spider, most notably chrome side-mouldings and fuller wings.*

BUGATTI TYPE 55
SUPER SPORT

In praise of style

The Bugatti Type 55 is to the Type 51 what the Type 43 was to the Type 35: a genuine grand tourer directly derived from a Grand Prix car. Announced at the 1931 Paris Motor Show, it was a canny amalgam of parts. The chassis used the members intended for the still-born 'double-eight' twin-supercharged 16-cylinder Type 47, the gearbox came from the Type 49, the clutch and the suspension from the Type 51, the brakes and wheels from the Type 43. The front end was new, however, with a dropped axle to allow a dynamo to be fitted in front of the engine.

The Type 55 also shared its magnificent engine with the Type 51: it thus had the same 2.3-litre capacity, the same twin-cam configuration with two inclined valves per cylinder, the same Roots-type supercharger. The only difference was that the output was kept down to 140bhp, rather than the 180bhp of the GP car. With this power unit the Type 55 was easily capable of over 110mph, which was remarkable for an early-1930s road car.

The styling was the work of Jean Bugatti, Ettore's son – a young Bugatti (then 22 years old) who was impetuous and romantic in character. The elegant and sophisticated Type 55 was made in his image. Even at this stage his artistic talents were given full rein in the creation of the car's sensual lines. The profile of the wings is in particular quite exemplary: they comprise a flow of curves uninterrupted by any straight line, even at the running boards, and continue over the rear wheels without a break. At the front the wings broaden out and suspend their movement

▲ *In theory Bugatti also offered the Type 55 as a coupé, but only a handful of cars were made. This example (chassis 55206) is preserved in Switzerland.*

in space. The colour scheme completes the effect, curves and mouldings highlighting the play of contrasting colours – black against the bright red, blue or yellow tints contained in the masterful scalloping of the car's sides.

The great majority of Type 55s were bodied at the factory, as a stripped-out door-less roadster; only very rarely were chassis entrusted to an outside coachbuilder. Worthy of note, all the same, is the sixth chassis (No. 55206), which was bodied as a cabriolet, with doors, by Lyons-based Billeter & Cartier; Gangloff also created a few cabriolets. There was also an elegant convertible by Figoni

WHAT IS IT THAT DISTINGUISHES A ROAD-GOING BUGATTI TYPE 55 FROM A GRAND PRIX TYPE 51? THE STYLE, THE ELEGANCE OF ITS LINES, THE NOBILITY OF ITS STANCE – IN BRIEF, THE GENIUS OF JEAN BUGATTI.

(chassis 55221) which is currently in England. Alongside the roadster, Bugatti also offered a coupé, the first example being delivered in March 1932. This style remained a rarity: there are three examples (chassis 55203, 55204, 55212) in the National Museum in Mulhouse (the former Schlumpf collection) and one (chassis 55206) in the collection of Charles Renaud.

In all, only 48 Bugatti Type 55 Super Sports were made.

▲ *The Type 55's contrasting sweeps of colour are very much part of Jean Bugatti's styling vocabulary. The car has always been a star of concours d'élégance, such as here, at Bagatelle in 1994.*

TECHNICAL SPECIFICATION

CONFIGURATION	FRONT ENGINE; RWD
STRUCTURE	SEPARATE LADDER CHASSIS
ENGINE	8-CYLINDER IN-LINE
VALVEGEAR	TWIN OVERHEAD CAMSHAFTS
CAPACITY	2,262CC (60MM X 100MM)
POWER	140BHP
FUEL SYSTEM	ZENITH/SOLEX CARBURETTOR; ROOTS SUPERCHARGER
GEARBOX	4-SPEED
WHEELBASE & TRACK	275CM; 125CM FRONT AND REAR
WEIGHT	800KG (BARE CHASSIS)
TYRES	29 X 5
MAXIMUM SPEED	112MPH (180KPH)
NUMBER BUILT	48
CHASSIS NUMBERS	55201 TO 55248

DELAHAYE 135 COMPÉTITION

For the greater good of the coachbuilding trade

The Type 135 turned Delahaye's image on its head. With the arrival of the '135' it was all over for austere bodywork, insipid models, and half-hearted mechanicals. With the Type 135, Delahaye all of a sudden rejoined the elite of the French motor industry, alongside Bugatti, Delage and Talbot.

The revolution took place in the setting of the 1935 Paris Motor Show. Derived from the Type 138, the Type 135 chassis was the work of engineer Jean François, an intelligent man who didn't stray from the orthodox, but took care to hone both the technology and the proportions of his raw material. Jean François knew how to tease out that extra dose of panache that led to a true classic, and the fundamental difference between the '135' and the '168' was the designed-in possibility of developing more sporting models, thanks to a low-slung chassis and the creation of a range of different power units.

▲ *After the Second World War, Figoni & Falaschi's striking creation still cut a striking figure in concours d'élégance.*

▶ *This 135 Compétition (chassis 48667) was one of the stars of the 1995* Automobiles Classiques *concours at Bagatelle.*

The Type 135 played a key part in the history of Delahaye. Part of a prolific range, it reached its zenith with the 'Compétition' chassis clothed by Figoni & Falaschi.

DELAHAYE 135 COMPÉTITION 1935 • 1939

▲ *Peter Mullin, owner of this 135 Compétition (chassis 49150), is an American collector particularly fond of the work of French coachbuilders.*

TECHNICAL SPECIFICATION

CONFIGURATION	FRONT ENGINE; RWD
STRUCTURE	SEPARATE CHASSIS
COACHWORK	STEEL
ENGINE	6-CYLINDER IN-LINE
VALVEGEAR	PUSHROD OVERHEAD-VALVE
CAPACITY	3,557CC (84MM X 107MM)
POWER	120BHP AT 4,200RPM (COMPÉTITION) 152BHP AT 4,300RPM (SPÉCIAL)
FUEL SYSTEM	3 SOLEX CARBURETTORS
GEARBOX	4-SPEED COTAL
WHEELBASE & TRACK	295CM; 138CM/148.5CM 270CM; 138CM/135CM (SWB)
WEIGHT	935KG (BARE CHASSIS)
TYRES	5.50 X 17
MAXIMUM SPEED	96–118MPH (155-190KPH)
NUMBER MADE	453 COMPÉTITIONS, PLUS 30 SWB COMPÉTITIONS AND 16 SPÉCIALS

For the 1936–38 model years the range coalesced around two series. On the one hand there were two cars with 3.2-litre engines, the 95bhp single-carb 135 Sport and the 110bhp triple-carb 135 Coupe des Alpes; on the other hand were two models with their engine taken out to 3.5 litres, the 120bhp 135 Compétition and the 152bhp short-chassis 135 Spécial.

It was with this last-named that the career of the Delahaye Type 135 took off. The 135 Spécial was conceived to satisfy the demands of the Automobile Club de France as far as sports-car racing was concerned. Fewer than 20 were built – in all likelihood only 16 – and most of them were given a lightweight cycle-winged body by Figoni & Falaschi. In this rudimentary guise the 135 Spécial was soon displaying its aptitude in all sorts of different conditions: it was as capable of winning in the snows of the Monte Carlo Rally (in 1937) as on the tarmac of Le Mans (in 1938).

Indeed, the Delahaye 135 Spécial can claim to be one of the most versatile cars in history, all the more so given that alongside its shows of sporting prowess it also shone in concours d'élégance. All the main coachbuilders made use of the 135 chassis, with Henri Chapron, Guilloré and Figoni & Falaschi being Delahaye's accredited partners. The offerings of Figoni & Falaschi were predictably the most flamboyant, the Boulogne-sur-Seine workshops producing a series of roadsters based on a design by illustrator Géo Ham, with fully-enclosed wings inspired by the landing-gear housings of a much-admired plane of the time, René Couzinet's Arc-en-Ciel. The first example was displayed at the 1936 Paris *salon* in an exuberant pink and orange livery; it caught the eye of the Aga Khan, who bought it a few weeks later after having had it repainted in more sober colours. Ten other roadsters, dubbed *phaétons grand sport*, were built to the same design theme, generally on a special short-wheelbase Compétition chassis.

For 1939 the Type 135 range was simplified, and based around two models, the 100bhp 135M Compétition and the 135bhp 135M Spécial (or MS) with an aluminium cylinder head.

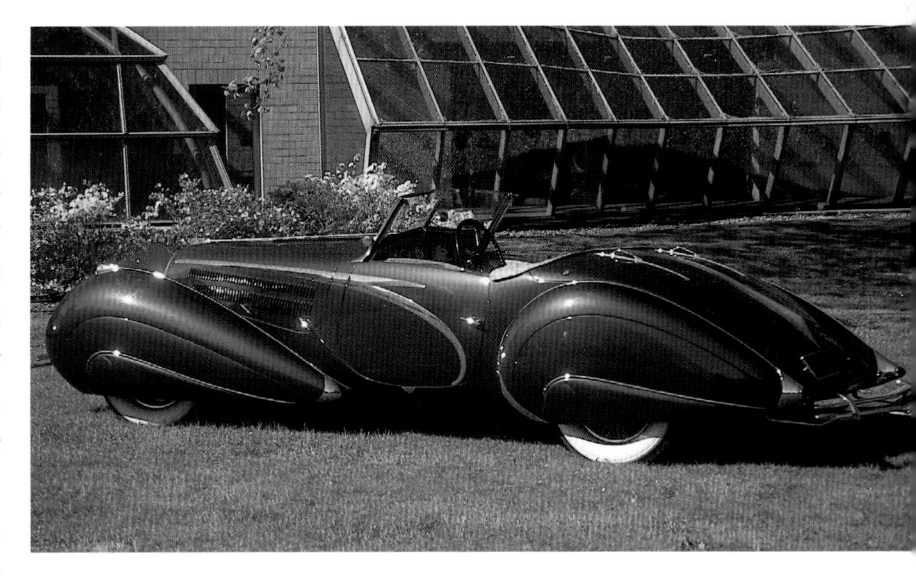

▲ *Peter Mullin's Delahaye 135 Compétition was much admired at the 2003 Villa d'Este concours.*

THE ELEVEN FIGONI & FALASCHI DELAHAYE 135 PHAETON GRAND SPORTS

1. 135 COMPÉTITION
DELIVERY: *October 1936*
REGISTRATION: *111-RK6 (France)*
BODYWORK: *Short chassis. Integral headlamps; single-blade bumpers. Smokey-pink paint with orange wings*
FIRST OWNER: *Ali Khan*
HISTORY: *Paris Motor Show, 1936*
LAST KNOWN SITUATION: *Chassis in US*

2. 135 COMPÉTITION
DELIVERY: *December 1936*
REGISTRATION: *2839-RK7*
BODYWORK: *Short chassis. Integral headlamps; double-blade bumpers. Smokey-pink paint with bordeaux wings*
FIRST OWNER: *Ali Amar*
HISTORY: *Brussels Motor Show, 1937*
LAST KNOWN SITUATION: *Probably disappeared*

3. 135
DELIVERY: *February 1937*
REGISTRATION: *5182-RK8*
BODYWORK: *Long chassis. Integral headlamps; twin-blade bumpers. Emerald green paint*
FIRST OWNER: *Pierre Barreaud de Lacour*
LAST KNOWN SITUATION: *Probably disappeared*

4. 135 COMPÉTITION
DELIVERY: *June 1937*
REGISTRATION: *44-RL1 then 9109-RP1 (France)*
BODYWORK: *Short chassis. Grey paintwork with blue mouldings*
FIRST OWNER: *Mr Perrin*
HISTORY: *Enghien concours, 1940s*
LAST KNOWN SITUATION: *Probably disappeared*

5. 135 COMPÉTITION No. 48666
DELIVERY: *1937*
BODYWORK: *Short chassis. Integral headlamps; single-blade bumpers. Pale grey paint with red wings*
FIRST OWNER: *Hoffman & Huppert (Austria)*
HISTORY: *Pebble Beach concours, 2000 (Best of Show)*
LAST KNOWN OWNER: *Jacques Harguindéguy*

6. 135 COMPÉTITION No. 48667
DELIVERY: *1937*
BODYWORK: *Short chassis. Integral headlamps. Yellow paint with marine blue wings*
FIRST OWNER: *Unknown*
LAST KNOWN OWNER: *Malcolm Pray (Connecticut)*

7. 135 COMPÉTITION No. 49150
DELIVERY: *October 1938*
BODYWORK: *Headlamps originally integral but now free-standing. Red paint, but now metallic dark blue*
FIRST OWNER: *Mr Jourde, Bombay (India)*
HISTORY: *Villa d'Este concours, 2003*
LAST KNOWN OWNER: *Peter Mullin (US)*

8. 135 COMPÉTITION No. 49169
DELIVERY: *March 1938*
REGISTRATION: *3230-AL15*
BODYWORK: *Long chassis. Integral headlamps; double-blade bumpers. Black paint*
FIRST OWNER: *Mr Migliacco (Algiers)*
LAST KNOWN SITUATION: *Peterson Museum (US)*

9. 135 MS No. 60217
DELIVERY: *1939*
BODYWORK: *Free-standing headlamps. Red paint*
FIRST OWNER: *In India*
LAST KNOWN OWNER: *Dalip Singh (India)*

10. 135 MS No. 60220
DELIVERY: *1939*
BODYWORK: *Integral headlamps. Black paint*
FIRST OWNER: *Mr Talma-Levadour*
LAST KNOWN OWNER: *Nobuo Harada (Japan)*

11. 135
DELIVERY DATE: *Unknown*
REGISTRATION: *1380-NH5 (France, 1948)*
COACHWORK: *Free-standing headlamps; simplified grille*
FIRST OWNER: *Unknown*
HISTORY: *Biarritz concours, 1940s*
LAST KNOWN SITUATION: *Probably disappeared*

The list of 135s carrying bodywork designed by Géo Ham includes a twelfth car (the fourth made), which was a 135 Compétition with coupé coachwork on a long-wheelbase chassis; it was delivered in May 1937.

1936

DELAGE D6-70 GRAND SPORT

TECHNICAL SPECIFICATION

CONFIGURATION	FRONT ENGINE; RWD
STRUCTURE	SEPARATE CHASSIS
ENGINE	6-CYLINDER IN-LINE
VALVEGEAR	PUSHROD OVERHEAD-VALVE
CAPACITY	2,984CC (83.7MM X 72.9MM)
POWER	120BHP AT 4,500RPM
FUEL SYSTEM	3 SOLEX CARBURETTORS
GEARBOX	4-SPEED COTAL
WHEELBASE & TRACK	270CM/146CM FRONT AND REAR
WEIGHT	1,080KG
TYRES	5.50 X 18IN
MAXIMUM SPEED	116MPH (186KPH)

▲ *This unique and gorgeous coupé having disappeared without trace, Auto Classique Touraine reconstituted the entire vehicle.*

To escape from the downward spiral, Delage rebuilt its image. It all kicked off in wonderful ambiguity, with a D6-70 that was as at home on the track at Le Mans as on the lawns of Longchamps.

Beauty and the beast

In the mid-thirties Delage was on the ropes, and Louis Delage was forced to file for bankruptcy on 10 April 1935. A British businessman, Walter Watney, also the main Delage concessionnaire in Paris, undertook a rescue operation. He bought the company's shares, wiped the debts off the slate, and on 15 July 1935 became the owner of the marque. He then passed Delahaye the manufacturing rights for Delage cars, while himself remaining at the head of the Société Nouvelle des Automobiles Delage.

Henceforth the name of the game was to establish two complementary ranges sharing the maximum number of mechanical components. At the 1935 Paris show Delage centred its efforts around the D6-70, directly derived from the previous year's D6-65. The engineer responsible, Arthur Michelat, more commonly known as Léon Michelat, therefore chose a Delahaye six-cylinder engine, bored out from 2.5 litres to 3 litres. From this was developed a much more sporting version for 1936's Le Mans, on chassis 50688, with Figoni and Falaschi finishing the splendid closed coupé coachwork in May of that year. Alas, the race was cancelled, on account of the strikes then paralysing France. Delage hoped to make up for lost ground at the French Grand Prix of 28 June…but the regulations excluded closed cars.

The only thing left for the beautiful fastback was for it to be shown off at the season's concours d'élégance. The Delage's first appearance was on 25 June 1936 at the *L'Auto* concours in the Bois de Boulogne, where it was presented by Mme Richer-Delaveau, wife of a garage-owner in Rue Bayard, in Paris. The car was then seen walking the boards at Le Touquet, Vichy, Deauville and Biarritz during the summer.

Racy, compact and untainted by needless frills, the Delage had the elegance of a true thoroughbred – and it wasn't long before it showed its mettle. Louis Gérard, a businessman and gentleman driver, bought the car and entered it for Le Mans. The Delage was stripped of its scant ornamentation and its rear spats, and ran as car number 19. Partnered by Jacques de Valance, Gérard finished fourth, an achievement that led to his being included in the official Delage team for 1938. The car then reappeared in the Paris–Nice rally and the Coupe de l'Automne at Montlhéry in summer 1937.

In 1938 the bodywork, which was felt to be too heavy, was put to one side and a lighter open shell built by Figoni. The original coupé coachwork was then mounted on a Delahaye 135 Spécial (chassis 47192) and entered in the 1938 Paris–Nice by Germaine Rouault. Meanwhile the now open Delage contested Le Mans in the hands of Louis Gérard and Jacques de Valence. Unfortunately the car retired, but in compensation it later won the Tourist Trophy. As for the original closed coachwork, that was again removed from its host chassis after the war, and disappeared for ever. In 2002 the car was reconstituted by Auto Classique Touraine.

▶ *Delage D6-70 Grand Sport chassis 50688 began its life in concours d'élégance.*

1936 ■ 1939

BUGATTI TYPE 57S

Crowning glory

Bugatti didn't delay in developing a sports version of the Type 57 it had launched at the 1933 Paris show: within two years the Type 57S had arrived. But the project only really came into its own when the first 57S-based Atalante made its appearance. The modifications made to the chassis were sufficient to transform the Type 57's silhouette. Not least, the bonnet-line was substantially lowered to accentuate the aggressive sporting nature of the Atalante, the flat horseshoe radiator shell being replaced by a vee'd oval unit. The 57S was shortened by a foot relative to the normal Type 57; it was also lowered thanks to the rear axle now passing through the chassis sidemembers rather than sitting below them. The 57S used De Ram dampers with pierced arms; at the front they were mounted on the engine and not on the chassis. The twin-cam 3.3-litre straight-eight, finally, had a dry sump, and was available with (57SC) or without (57S) a supercharger.

The official launch was at the 1936 Paris *salon*, the Atalante coupé being exhibited alongside an experimental Type 57S roadster and the pontoon-bodied 57G competition *tank* which had won that year's French GP. The pale green roadster had stripped-down door-less coachwork, with the front wheels totally enclosed by helmet-type wings the front element of which pivoted with the wheels. After the show the car was given orthodox wings and sold to painter André Derain, and in 1952 it was completely re-bodied, in a more ordinary style, by coachbuilder Tunesi. Recently the car was recreated in its original form, for exhibition in California's Behring Museum.

The most numerous of the 42 examples of the 57S built were those with Atalante bodywork – at least 15 are known, including chassis 57375, 57383, 57384, 57441, 57451, 57471, 57481, 57492, 57502, 57511, 57532, and 57592. But several other coachbuilders had a go, and there are at least three Vanvooren cabriolets (57482, 57513 and 57571) and three by Vanden Plas of England (57512, 57541 and 57572). Less well-known, but remarkable all the same, are the cars created by Corsica Coachworks Ltd, who attained the summit of their art with their work on the 57S. Established in 1920 in Highbury, in North London, Corsica

▶ *Lower and shorter than the other Type 57s, the Type 57S gave birth to various more sporting styles of body. This drophead, on chassis 57563 of August 1937, is by Gangloff.*

WITH THE BUGATTI TYPE 57S, EVERY MODEL WAS MORE EXCLUSIVE THAN THE ONE BEFORE. BUT MOST MYTHICAL OF ALL WAS THE LEGENDARY ATLANTIC.

BUGATTI 57S
1936 • 1939

▲ *The second Atlantic built (57453) went to racing-driver 'Williams'.*

TECHNICAL SPECIFICATION	
CONFIGURATION	FRONT ENGINE; RWD
STRUCTURE	SEPARATE LADDER CHASSIS
ENGINE	8-CYLINDER IN-LINE
VALVEGEAR	TWIN OVERHEAD CAMSHAFTS
CAPACITY	3,257CC (72MM X 100MM)
POWER	175BHP/200BHP
FUEL SYSTEM	STROMBERG UUR2 CARBURETTOR; OPTIONAL SUPERCHARGER (57SC)
GEARBOX	4-SPEED
WHEELBASE & TRACK	298CM; 125CM FRONT AND REAR
WEIGHT	1,250KG (ATLANTIC)
TYRES	5.50 X 18IN FRONT; 6.00 X 18IN REAR
MAXIMUM SPEED	110/120MPH (175/200KPH)
NUMBER BUILT	42, OF WHICH 3 ATLANTIC
CHASSIS NUMBERS	55201–55248

first came up with a roadster (57375), used by gentleman driver Embiricos in the August 1936 Tourist Trophy. This was followed by a cabriolet (57491) for another amateur racing-driver, TASO Mathieson, and by a very British-looking roadster (57531), registered DYF4, for Sir Malcolm Campbell. The crème de la crème, though, was the final car, the roadster (57593) designed by Eric Giles and delivered in February 1938 to his brother Geoffrey. Today the property of John Mozart, this sublime creation – originally registered GU 7 – was awarded 'Best of Show' at the 1998 Pebble Beach concours.

▲ *The Atalante coachwork really came into its own on the short-chassis 57S.*

The most mythical of all: the Type 57 Atlantic

The most mythical of all 57S models, of all 57s, and probably of all Bugattis, left Molsheim at the same time as the first Atalante, but was not exhibited at the 1936 Paris show. It picked up on the lines of the Aérolithe seen at the 1935 *salon*, and was, of course, the famous Atlantic – a car whose extreme rarity and singular beauty are the stuff of legend.

Once again, the talent of Jean Bugatti expressed itself in an innate sense of proportion, and with all ornamentation suppressed in favour of a strictly technological aesthetic language. This originality of approach was symbolised by the riveted flanges running over the roof and down to the tail, and forming the peaks to the front and rear wings.

Only three examples were sold, at a price of 117,000 francs (against 109,000 francs for an Atalante coupé), and three are in existence today, although one is a total reconstruction.

▲ *One of the most beautiful 57S styles is almost certainly this roadster built in England by Corsica (chassis 57593). Right: the third Atlantic made (57591).*

THE THREE BUGATTI ATLANTICS

1. No. 57374
DELIVERY: *September 1936*
REGISTRATION: *6559 WW 20*
BODYWORK: *Low-set headlamps; scuttle-mounted trafficators; chromed 'comet' bonnet side-trims*
ORIGINAL OWNER: *Lord Rothschild (GB)*
LAST KNOWN OWNER: *Peter Williamson (US)*

2. No. 57453
DELIVERY: *December 1936*
REGISTRATION: *5800 NV3*
BODYWORK: *Low-set headlamps; rear stoneguards; side wind-deflectors. Modified after the war, destroyed in an accident in 1955, and recreated in the 1980s by Carrosserie Lecoq; today in aubergine paint*
ORIGINAL OWNER: William Grover ('Williams')
HISTORY: *Paris-Nice, 1936; Nice salon, 1936*
LAST KNOWN OWNER: *Michel Seydoux (France)*

3. No. 57374
DELIVERY: *May 1938*
REGISTRATION: *EXK 6 (GB)*
BODYWORK: *High-set torpedo-shell headlamps; unspatted rear wheels; currently in black paint*
ORIGINAL OWNER: *M.R. Pope (GB)*
HISTORY: *Pebble Beach, 1990 ('Best of Show')*
LAST KNOWN OWNER: *Ralph Lauren (US)*

1937 – 1939

TALBOT LAGO T150C
SUPER SPORT

THE FRENCH CALLED THEM 'GOUTTE D'EAU' – IN ENGLISH WE'D CALL THEM 'TEARDROP'. BUT CALL THEM WHAT YOU WILL, THESE COUPÉS WITH THEIR FIGONI & FALASCHI COACHWORK ARE THE MOST BEAUTIFUL TALBOT SUPER SPORTS OF ALL.

A few drops of splendour

At the 1936 Paris Motor Show Talbot announced a new grand tourer called the Lago-Spécial Grand Sport, powered by a 4-litre engine in either a normal (2.95m wheelbase) chassis or in a shortened (2.65m wheelbase) form. A few months later the swb version was renamed 'Super Sport' or 'SS'. In its essentials the Talbot Lago SS borrowed the chassis of the T150C racer which had been campaigned in the 1936 season.

For the 1937 *salon* the Lago SS was represented by a Figoni & Falaschi roadster, but then a few weeks later, at the New York show, opening on 27 October, Talbot displayed an extraordinary 'aerodynamic coupé'. The car was soon known as the 'New York', in acknowledgement of its debut. Finally, Figoni & Falaschi developed a second design in the same vein; officially the '9221', the new style ended up being known as the 'Jeancart', after the name of the initial car's first owner. On this variant the side windows were not quite as oval and the boot formed more of a separate volume than on the more flowing 'New York'. All these cars became known as the 'gouttes d'eau', an informal appellation which suits them admirably…

Of the 25 examples of the Lago T150C-SS, a few did not have Figoni & Falaschi coachwork. In particular, Pourtout of Rueil-Malmaison created a small run of four magnificent coupés styled by Georges Paulin, on chassis 90119 to 90122, while

◀ *Chassis 90103, preserved in the US, is one of the ten 'teardrop' Talbots with 'New York' coachwork.*

TECHNICAL SPECIFICATION	
CONFIGURATION	FRONT ENGINE; RWD
STRUCTURE	SEPARATE CHASSIS
BODYWORK	STEEL
ENGINE	6-CYLINDER IN-LINE
VALVEGEAR	PUSHROD OHV; HEMI HEAD
CAPACITY	3,996CC (90MM X 104.5MM)
POWER	140BHP AT 4,100RPM, 200BHP AT 4,800RPM
FUEL SYSTEM	TRIPLE 35MM ZENITH CARBURETTORS
GEARBOX	WILSON PRE-SELECTOR
WHEELBASE & TRACK	265CM; 132CM FRONT AND REAR
WEIGHT	850KG (BARE CHASSIS)
TYRES	5.50 X 17IN
MAXIMUM SPEED	106MPH (170KPH)
NUMBER BUILT	25 (ALL TYPES OF SS)
CHASSIS NUMBERS	90101 TO 90125

TALBOT LAGO T150C SUPER SPORT 1937 • 1939

▲ Philippe de Massa entered Lago SS chassis 90117 in 1939's Le Mans 24-Hours.

◀ A 'Jeancart' coupé (chassis 90104) on display at the 1992 Pebble Beach concours.

Talbot itself bodied chassis 90114, the car being delivered in July 1937 with the registration 2212-RL2.

But the fame of the Lago SS rests squarely on the 'teardrop' coupés. A key member of the baroque tendency in French coachbuilding, Figoni & Falaschi had the courage to combine simple forms with a certain ornamental overload. Yet despite a sometimes simplistic futurism and an often over-the-top sensuality, Figoni's flamboyant coachwork always had a gutsy seductiveness.

▲ *The 'Jeancart' is recognisable in profile by its three-box shape. This example was 'Best of Show' at the 1992 Bagatelle concours.*

THE 15 'TEARDROP' TALBOT LAGO T150CS

1. T150C No. 90101
DELIVERY: *April 1937*
REGISTRATION: *2270-RL1*
BODYWORK: *Type 9221 'Jeancart'; black with orange mouldings; restored in the 1980s*
FIRST OWNER: *M Jeancart*

2. T150C No. 90103
DELIVERY: *July 1937*
REGISTRATION: *9183-RL3*
BODYWORK: *Type 9220 'New York'; blue with grey wings; then two-tone blue*
FIRST OWNER: *Freddy McEvoy (US)*
HISTORY: *New York Motor Mhow, 1937*
LAST KNOWN OWNER: *William Marriott (US)*

3. T150C No. 90104
DELIVERY: *January 1938*
REGISTRATION: *U2UJBIEN*
BODYWORK: *Type 9221 'Jeancart'; aubergine paintwork; then marine blue with grey wings*
FIRST OWNER: *Fernand Masquefa (Algeria)*
HISTORY: *Bagatelle concours, 1992, and Pebble Beach 1993, 1997, 2000*
LAST KNOWN OWNER: *William E Connor*

4. T150C No. 90105
DELIVERY: *January 1937*
REGISTRATION: *9187-RL3*
BODYWORK: *Type 9220 'New York'; marine blue with grey wings; now red*
FIRST OWNER: *Tommy Lee (California)*
LAST KNOWN LOCATION: *United Kingdom*

5.T150C No. 90106
DELIVERY: *September 1937*
REGISTRATION: *9165-RL5*
BODYWORK: *Type 9220 'New York'; metallic grey paintwork; now aubergine*
FIRST OWNER: *Woolf Barnato (GB)*
HISTORY: *London Motor Show, 1937; Pebble Beach, 1990*
LAST KNOWN OWNER: *Peter Mullin (California)*

6. T150C No. 90107
DELIVERY: *1937*
REGISTRATION: *3772-RL4*
BODYWORK: *Type 9220 'New York'; grey body with blue wings*
FIRST OWNER: *Maharani Stella de Kapurthala*
HISTORY: *Concours d'élégance Fémina, June 1938*
LAST KNOWN OWNER: *Heirs to Lindley Locke (California)*

7. T150C No. 90108
DELIVERY: *1937*
BODYWORK: *Type 9220 'New York'; blue paintwork*
LAST KNOWN LOCATION: *Brooks Stevens Museum, 1950s*

8. T150C No. 90109
DELIVERY: *1938*
REGISTRATION: *9187-RL3*
BODYWORK: *Type 9220 'New York'; now in aubergine paint*
FIRST OWNER: *Robin Byng*
HISTORY: *Paris Motor Show, 1938*
LAST KNOWN LOCATION: *Rosso Bianco Collection (Germany)*

9. T150C No. 90110
DELIVERY: *1937*
REGISTRATION: *Unknown*
BODYWORK: *Type 9220 'New York'; rebodied by Graber c.1946, then given replica '9220' body in 2003 by ACT; now black with silver-grey wings*
HISTORY: *Rétromobile, 2003*
LAST KNOWN LOCATION: *Belgium*

10. T150C No. 90112
DELIVERY: *May 1938*
REGISTRATION: *9120-RL7*
BODYWORK: *Type 92 20 'New York'; black paintwork*
FIRST OWNER: *M Toussaint (Belgium)*
HISTORY: *Concours de L'Auto, Paris, June 1939*
LAST KNOWN LOCATION: *Belgium*

11. T150C No. 90115
DELIVERY: *May 1938*
REGISTRATION: *796 CA 76*
BODYWORK: *Figoni & Falaschi cabriolet; blue with dark blue wings*
LAST KNOWN LOCATION: *Private collection*

12. T150YC No. 90116
DELIVER: *May 1938*
REGISTRATION: *9914-RL7*
BODYWORK: *Type 9221 'Jeancart'; blue paintwork*
HISTORY: *Le Mans, 1938 (car No. 5)*

13. T150C No. 90117
DELIVERY: *October 1938*
REGISTRATION: *9410-RM*
BODYWORK: *Type 9220 'New York'; silver-grey paintwork*
FIRST OWNER: *Philippe de Massa*
HISTORY: *Le Mans, 1939 (car no. 8)*
LAST KNOWN LOCATION: *California*

14. T150C No. 90121 (or 90034)
DELIVERY: *May 1938*
REGISTRATION: *1938 KB 13*
BODYWORK: *Type 9221 'Jeancart'; dark blue paintwork*
FIRST OWNER: *Philippe de Massa*
LAST KNOWN LOCATION: *Europe*

15. T150C No. 90123
DELIVERY: *1938*
REGISTRATION: *Unknown*
BODYWORK: *Type 9220 'New York', recently reconstructed by ACT; now black*
LAST KNOWN LOCATION: *France*

Figoni & Falaschi also built several cabriolets along similar lines, including chassis 90115. The Boulogne-sur-Seine coachbuilder was also responsible for a roadster on a racing chassis (T105C No. 82928), registered 6694-RK5; this was shown at Pebble Beach in 2002 by James A. Paterson.

ALFA ROMEO
8C 2900 B

The revival of Italian coachbuilding

Just as with its predecessor at Alfa Romeo, the 8C 2900 had a career that intimately combined motoring for sport and motoring for leisure. Although its name first appeared in the catalogues in September 1934, the story of the 8C 2900 only really began in October 1935. On the Paris Motor Show stand that month could be seen the model that was to take over from the glorious 8C 2300, star of four Le Mans victories in 1931, 1932, 1933 and 1934. Under the glass dome of the Grand Palais, with its sumptuous Pierre Granet décor, could be seen chassis number 412001, carrying open sports 'factory' coachwork and road equipment. A few months later the 8C 2900 showed its other face, with its competition baptism in the 1936 Mille Miglia. For this purpose it was in an altogether more rudimentary guise, with simplified bodywork based on that of the Grand Prix 8C 35 racers and called *botticella* – or 'little barrel'. This first competition outing was stunning: the three cars entered finished 1-2-3!

Keeping up the momentum, Alfa Romeo ran off a small series of spider-bodied cars in the same style as the Paris show car (chassis 412002, 412006, 412010, 412013, 412015); Zagato bodied another spider (chassis 412011) for the 1937

▶ *Touring's spider on the short-chassis 8C 2900 B is one of the masterpieces of Italian coachbuilding. This car (chassis 412014) was displayed at the 1937 Milan Motor Show.*

TECHNICAL SPECIFICATION	
CONFIGURATION	FRONT ENGINE; RWD
STRUCTURE	SEPARATE CHASSIS AND TUBULAR FRAME; ALUMINIUM PANELS
ENGINE	8-CYLINDER IN-LINE
VALVEGEAR	TWIN OVERHEAD CAMSHAFTS
CAPACITY	2,905CC (68MM X 100MM)
POWER	180BHP AT 2,500RPM
FUEL SYSTEM	TWIN HORIZONTAL CARBURETTORS; TWIN SUPERCHARGERS
GEARBOX	4-SPEED
WHEELBASE & TRACK	280CM/300CM; 135CM FRONT AND REAR
WEIGHT	1,150KG/1,250KG
TYRES	5.50 X 19IN
MAXIMUM SPEED	115MPH (185KPH)
NUMBER BUILT	43 (OF WHICH 21 SWB)
CHASSIS NUMBERS	412001 TO 412043

AT THE PEAK OF ITS ART, TOURING BUILT SEVERAL SERIES OF INFINITELY DESIRABLE CARS ON THE 8C 2900 CHASSIS – HIGH-SOCIETY OUT-TAKES FROM ALFA'S SPORTING HERITAGE.

ALFA ROMEO 8C 2900 B 1937 • 1939

THE FIVE LONG-WHEELBASE ALFA ROMEO 8C 2900 BERLINETTAS BODIED BY TOURING

1. CHASSIS No. 412020 DELIVERY: *October 1937* REGISTRATION: *MI 65119 (Italy)* HISTORY: *Paris and Milan motor shows, 1937* LAST KNOWN OWNER: *Mike Sparken* **2. CHASSIS No. 412024** DELIVERY: *1937* REGISTRATION: *FLR 108 (GB)* FIRST OWNER: *Jack Bartlett (London)* HISTORY: The Autocar *(August 1949)* LAST KNOWN OWNER: *Jan Martens (Netherlands)*	**3. CHASSIS No. 412029** DELIVERY: *1937* REGISTRATION: *LU-1511 (Switzerland)* BODYWORK: *Blue-Grey* FIRST OWNER: *Swiss* LAST KNOWN OWNER: *Alfa Romeo collection, Arese*	**4. CHASSIS No. 412035** DELIVERY: *August 1938* REGISTRATION TODAY: *DXH 497T (South Africa)* BODYWORK: *Marine Blue* FIRST OWNER: *Mr Donegani (Italy)* HISTORY: *Pebble Beach concours, 1994* LAST KNOWN OWNER: *David Cohen (South Africa)*	**5. CHASSIS No. 412035** DELIVERY: *September 1938* REGISTRATION: *MI-67370 (Italy)* BODYWORK: *Red* FIRST OWNER: *Unknown* HISTORY: *Paris Motor Show, 1938; Mille Miglia, 1948 (First)* LAST KNOWN OWNER: *Paul Moser (California); sold at Carmel, August 2002*

◀ *This long-wheelbase berlinetta (chassis 412035) is currently kept in the Alfa Romeo collection in Arese.*

Milan show, while Pinin Farina came up with two extraordinary cabriolets – chassis 412004, which was an entrant in the May 1939 Nice concours d'élégance, and chassis 412012, which was a latter-day star at the 1992 Bagatelle concours. Meanwhile, Stabilimenti Farina, run by a breakaway branch of the family, came up with a somewhat less attractive spider in November 1938, on chassis 412028. All these various cars were on a short-wheelbase chassis.

Over and above these masterstrokes, the creative genius most closely linked to the Alfa Romeo 8C 2900 will always be Carrozzeria Touring. The firm unveiled its first long-wheelbase berlinetta at the 1937 Paris show. Three weeks later, in Milan, at the end of October, came its open spider built on the short-wheelbase chassis. Finally, in 1938, Touring translated the lines of its spider to the long-wheelbase car. These three models between them constitute the very summit of Italian coachwork art.

THE SIX SHORT-WHEELBASE ALFA ROMEO 8C 2900 SPIDERS BODIED BY TOURING

1. CHASSIS No. 412014
DELIVERY: *October 1937*
REGISTRATION: *SUB 95-47 (New York)*
BODYWORK: *Today black with red interior*
FIRST OWNER: *Mr McClure Halley (US)*
HISTORY: *Milan Motor Show, 1937; Bagatelle concours, 1996 (Best of Show)*
LAST KNOWN OWNER: *John Mozart (US)*

2. CHASSIS No. 412016
DELIVERY: *April 1938*
REGISTRATION: *0420 Roma*
BODYWORK: *Today red*
FIRST OWNER: *Prince Bernhard of the Netherlands*
LAST KNOWN OWNER: *Jim Ibold (Cincinnati, US)*

3. CHASSIS No. 412017
DELIVERY: *March 1938*
REGISTRATION: *TO 49700 (Italy)*
FIRST OWNER: *Piergiuseppe Gurgo-Salice*
HISTORY: *Turin concours d'élégance, 1938*

4. CHASSIS No. 412018
DELIVERY: *Unknown*
BODYWORK: *Today grey with red detailing*
FIRST OWNER: *Jean Studer (Switzerland)*
HISTORY: *Pebble Beach concours, 2002*
LAST KNOWN OWNER: *Robert Bahre (Maine, US)*

5. CHASSIS No. 412019
DELIVERY: *1938*
REGISTRATION: *NS-2*
BODYWORK: *Today yellow with red detailing and interior*
FIRST OWNER: *Maharajah of Indore*
LAST KNOWN OWNER: *Tom Perkins (California)*

6. CHASSIS No. 412021
DELIVERY: *1938*
REGISTRATION: *KB 000 225 (Germany)*
BODYWORK: *Cutaway front wings*
HISTORY: Auto Motor und Sport, *c.1946*

ALFA ROMEO 8C 2900 B 1937 • 1939

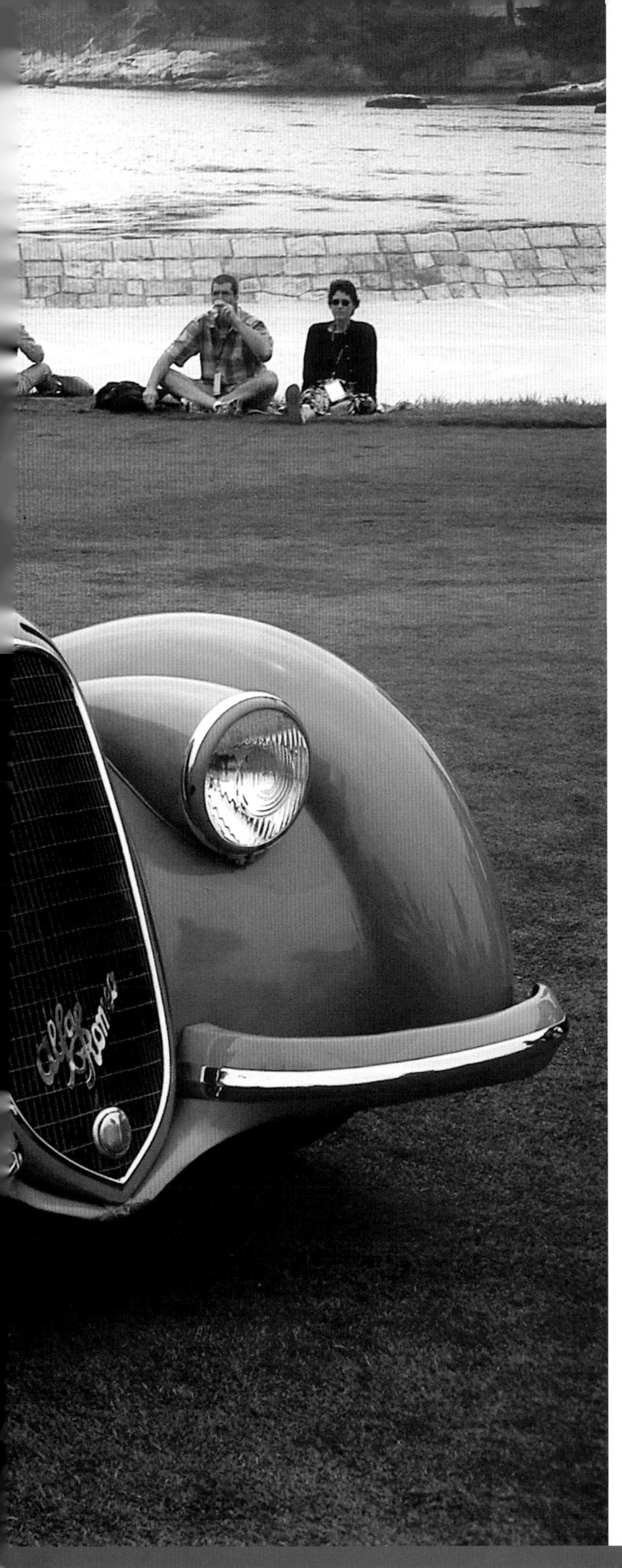

◀ *Unornamented lines and elegant proportions characterise the style of Touring's spider. This example, on swb chassis 412018, is in superbly original condition.*

THE SEVEN LONG-WHEELBASE ALFA ROMEO 8C 2900 SPIDERS BODIED BY TOURING

1. No. 412022
DELIVERY: *Summer 1939*
REGISTRATION: *KPE 842 (GB)*
BODYWORK: *Currently red*
FIRST OWNER: *Thompson & Taylor (Surrey)*
HISTORY: *Pebble Beach concours, 1985*
LAST KNOWN OWNER: *John Mozart (US)*

2. No. 412023
DELIVERY: *Unknown*
REGISTRATION: *BE 2267 (Switzerland)*
BODYWORK: *Red*
FIRST OWNER: *M. Schlatter (Switzerland)*
LAST KNOWN OWNER: *John North (Maryland)*

3. No. 412025
DELIVERY: *1938*
BODYWORK: *Unknown*
FIRST OWNER: *Unknown*
HISTORY: *London motor show, 1938*

4. No. 412026
DELIVERY: *February 1939*
REGISTRATION: *KHX 2 (GB)*
BODYWORK: *Red with black upholstery*
FIRST OWNER: *British*
HISTORY: *'Road & Track', May 1966*
LAST KNOWN LOCATION: *Luigi Chinetti collection (Connecticut)*

5. No. 412027
DELIVERY: *Unknown*
REGISTRATION: *Unknown*
BODYWORK: *Red; supplementary front grilles*
FIRST OWNER: *British*
LAST KNOWN LOCATION: *Fred Simeone collection (Philadelphia)*

6. No. 412040
DELIVERY: *Unknown*
REGISTRATION: *Roma 72440 (Italy)*
BODYWORK: *Red*
FIRST OWNER:*Partito Nazionale Fascista (Italian fascist party)*

7. No. 412041
DELIVERY: *Unknown*
REGISTRATION: *Unknown*
BODYWORK: *Red; supplementary front grilles*
FIRST OWNER: *British*
HISTORY: *Race in Buenos Aires, 1952*

Other than the examples listed here, Touring also bodied six spiders for the 1938 Mille Miglia (chassis numbers -030, -031, -032, -034, -037, -038) and one streamlined berlinetta (-033) for 1938's Le Mans 24-Hours.

1938 ■ 1946

DELAHAYE 165

THE RACE-BRED TWELVE-CYLINDER DELAHAYE WAS GIVEN THE TASK OF REPRESENTING FRENCH CREATIVITY AT THE 1939 NEW YORK TRADE FAIR.

Modernity with a French accent

New York, January 1939. America was marking the 150th anniversary of its democracy and the election of its first president by organising a celebration of the modern age. 'The World of Tomorrow' was the theme of this ambitious world fair in New York. The world of tomorrow; the slogan jars somewhat when over on the other side of the Atlantic the Second World War wasn't far away. But despite its troubles, Europe made its contribution to the futuristic dreams on display in New York.

Waving the flag for French elegance were two of its coachbuilders: Letourneur & Marchand, who despatched two D8-120 Delages, and rival Figoni & Falaschi, who sent a D8-120 cabriolet and a Delahaye 165 roadster. This last-named was similar to the car that had been shown at the 1938 Paris *salon*, on chassis 60743, with the same flamboyant coachwork that wavered between the classical and the baroque, between faux modernism and genuine panache. Somehow the Delahaye turned all its failings of taste to its advantage. The over-long profile gave it exuberance, the excessively sculpted wings underlined the car's power, and the over-wrought ornamentation gave it a slightly pathetic air, like a fading actress wearing just a little too much make-up for her own good. Yet despite its all-enveloping form, the design was in fact relatively conservative, with the wings, headlamps and grille still very much separate items.

◀ *Created for the 1939 New York World Fair, this extravagant Delahaye 165 (chassis 60744) has lived its entire life in the United States.*

TECHNICAL SPECIFICATION

CONFIGURATION	FRONT ENGINE; RWD
STRUCTURE	SEPARATE CHASSIS
ENGINE	V12 (60 DEG)
VALVEGEAR	1 CENTRAL CAMSHAFT AND TWO SIDE CAMSHAFTS
CAPACITY	4,496CC (75MM X 84.7MM)
POWER	175BHP AT 4,500RPM
FUEL SYSTEM	3 TWIN-CHOKE STROMBERG CARBURETTORS
GEARBOX	4-SPEED COTAL
WHEELBASE & TRACK	321CM; 141CM/149CM
WEIGHT	1,450KG
TYRES	7.00 X 17
MAXIMUM SPEED	120MPH (200KPH)
NUMBER MADE	4–5 ORIGINAL TYPE 165
CHASSIS NUMBERS	60741 TO 60744

DELAHAYE 165
1938 • 1946

▲ *The classical radiator doesn't really go with the baroque style of the Figoni body of '60744'.*

THE ROADGOING DELAHAYE V12s

1. 145/48772
DELIVERY: *June 1937*
BODYWORK: *Two-seat racer, re-bodied as coupé by Henri Chapron, 1945*
HISTORY: *French GP, 1937*
LAST KNOWN OWNER: *Hubertus Dönhoff (Germany)*

2. 145/48773
DELIVERY: *July 1937*
BODYWORK: *Two-seat racer, re-bodied as coupé by Henri Chapron, 1945*
HISTORY: *Marne GP, 1937*
LAST KNOWN LOCATION: *United States*

3. 145/48774
DELIVERY: *1937*
BODYWORK: *Two-seat racer, re-bodied as cabriolet by Franay, 1946*
HISTORY: *Million GP, 1937; Paris salon 1946 (Franay body)*
LAST KNOWN OWNER: *Behring Museum (California)*

4. 165/60741
DELIVERY: *August 1938*
BODYWORK: *Cabriolet by Henri Chapron*

5. 165/60742
DELIVERY: *Unknown*
BODYWORK: *Coupé*

6. 165/60743
DELIVERY: *October 1938*
BODYWORK: *Figoni & Falaschi roadster; marine blue paintwork*
FIRST OWNER: *W.E. Butlin (GB)*
HISTORY: *Paris Motor Show, 1938*
LAST KNOWN OWNER: *Robert Lee (Nevada)*

7. 165/60744
DELIVERY: *May 1938*
BODYWORK: *Figoni & Falaschi roadster; red paintwork*
HISTORY: *World Fair, New York, 1939*
LAST KNOWN OWNER: *Peter Mullin (US)*

The V12 engine was derived from the power unit used in the Type 145 and Type 155 that were campaigned in the GPs and endurance races of the 1937–39 period. Nobody in New York would hear that magnificent V12, though: the left-hand bonnet side was transparent, to show off the entrails of the machine, but the engine block was empty. There was neither crankshaft nor rods and pistons… When the curtain fell on the World Fair, the Delahaye didn't return to Europe. It was put in store before reappearing in 1946 at International Motors, a garage then employing two youngsters with a bright future ahead of them: World Champion of 1961 Phil Hill, and Bernard Cahier, to become a respected French motoring journalist. The car was eventually sold to a New York businessman who had a Cadillac V8 fitted so he could use the car. Later the car was abandoned at a farm in California.

At the beginning of the 1980s collector Jim Hull, a great lover of high-class French machinery, got wind of this abandoned car in a barn somewhere in California. He ended up persuading the cantankerous old farmer to sell him the wreck. All that was left was to find the original engine – or rather the empty shell of an engine that had been under the Delahaye's bonnet at the New York fair. This mock-up had finished up in the Type 145 Delahaye of Hubertus Dönhoff, in Germany. Armed with this, British specialists Crosthwaite & Gardiner were commissioned to make the missing components. The resuscitated vehicle had its debut at the 1992 Pebble Beach concours.

As for the Delahaye 165 on which the car was based, its career was interrupted by the Second World War. Other than the two Figoni & Falaschi roadsters of 1938, two – or possibly three – other chassis were bodied pre-war, according to *Le Grand Livre Delahaye* by Jean-Pierre Dauliac, Jacques Dorizon and François Peigney. Further to this, after the war three of the four Type 145 racers were re-bodied as roadgoing grand tourers – a couple as two-seat coupés by Chapron and a single car as a Franay cabriolet.

▼ *The 145 campaigned in the 1937 Million GP was given a new body by Franay in 1946.*

1948 · 1950

TALBOT LAGO T26
GRAND SPORT

From grand sport to great art

During the Second World War the management of Talbot made preparations for the future – proof of true optimism. The weapon of choice, according to Anthony Lago, would be a twin-cam 4.5-litre power unit, this engine size corresponding to Grand Prix rules but also to those of endurance racing, most particularly for Le Mans. At the same time Lago also sought to exploit the mechanicals for a high-perfomance grand tourer – an ideal base for the French coachbuilding industry, which at the time didn't seem to know where it was going.

The bare chassis of the T26 Grand Sport was unveiled at the 1947 Paris *salon*. At the same show a year later, the chassis could be found dressed in various styles. On its own stand Talbot displayed a coupé concocted at the factory: an awful thing, with awkward lines and an ugly front. At Saoutchik they rose to the same challenge with brio, impact and spirit, the Russian-born coachbuilder unveiling the first of six extravagantly-styled coupés. The baroque tendencies of the Neuilly-sur-Seine master-artist translated into pure panache. An extrovert and romantic Slav, Jacques Saoutchik truly melded exuberance with elegance. Indeed, Saoutchik coachwork was always extremely sophisticated, with overblown forms, exaggerated volumes and excessive ornamentation, yet avoiding aerodynamic

▶ *This T26 GS, by Franay (chassis 110 123) had a somewhat pudgy style.*

TECHNICAL SPECIFICATION	
CONFIGURATION	FRONT ENGINE; RWD
STRUCTURE	SEPARATE CHASSIS
BODYWORK	STEEL
ENGINE	6-CYLINDER IN-LINE
VALVEGEAR	TWIN HIGH-SET SIDE CAMSHAFTS
CAPACITY	4,482CC (93MM X 110MM)
POWER	190BHP AT 4,000RPM
WHEELBASE & TRACK	265CM; 139CM/133CM
WEIGHT	850KG (BARE CHASSIS)
MAXIMUM SPEED	118MPH (190KPH)
NUMBER BUILT	26
CHASSIS NUMBERS	110 101 TO 110 126

WITH THE WAR OVER, THE DREAM OF A MULTI-TALENTED CHASSIS, GOOD FOR ALL SPORTING DISCIPLINES, RESURFACED AT TALBOT. THE REALITY BEHIND THE DREAM WAS CALLED THE GRAND SPORT.

▲ *In spite of its exuberance, this Saoutchik creation on chassis 110 101 certainly doesn't lack elegance.*

extravagances. At the same time Jacques Saoutchik regretted 'the continual changes in the motor car, inspired by the American mentality'.

In all, Talbot only made 26 of the original short-chassis T26 GS, with its 2.65m wheelbase, this between (July) 1948 and 1950. Over and above those cars that followed the same design theme, Saoutchik produced some other less happy exercises. Then Henri Chapron, Figoni & Falaschi, Antem, Dubos (chassis 110 117) and Franay (chassis 110 123) came up with their interpretation of the same theme. Meanwhile, two cars stood out for their sporting career. One was a berlinetta by Contamin, on chassis 110 005, which ran at Le Mans in 1949 and 1950 in the hands of André Chambas; the other was chassis number 110 106, which was at first clothed by Vanden Plas before being re-bodied by Martial Oblin in 1951 for the Liège-Rome-Liège rally, and then being shown at the 1952 Brussels *salon*. So many designs, yet none eclipsed the extravagance of the Saoutchik cars…

▶ *The Lago Grand Sports bodied by Saoutchik (here chassis 110 111) were among the great stars of forties concours d'élégance.*

THE SIX TALBOT LAGO GRAND SPORT COUPÉS BODIED BY SAOUTCHIK

1. T26 GS No. 110 101
DELIVERY: *July 1948*
REGISTRATION: *230-RQ6*
BODYWORK: *Oval grille; two-tone green, then two-tone blue*
FIRST OWNER: *M. Bogey*
HISTORY: *Paris Motor Show, 1948; Pebble Beach, 1984*
LAST KNOWN OWNER: *Jacques Harguindéguy (California)*

2. T26 GS No. 110 109
DELIVERY: *November 1949*
REGISTRATION: *8-RS3*
BODYWORK: *Vertical grille; spatted wheels; black paint*

3. T26 GS No. 110 111
DELIVERY: *June 1951*
REGISTRATION: *1184-RQ9*
BODYWORK: *Vertical grille; spatted wheels; white paint*
HISTORY: *Enghien concours, June 1951*
LAST KNOWN OWNER: *Guido Bartolomeo (France)*

4. T26 GS No. 110 114
DELIVERY: *December 1948*
REGISTRATION TODAY: *1-RS5*
BODYWORK: *Vertical grille; spatted wheels; blue-grey metallic paint*
FIRST OWNER: *Clive Cussler*
HISTORY: *Enghien concours, 1949*
LAST KNOWN OWNER: *In United States*

5. T26 GS No. 110 116
DELIVERY: *1949*
REGISTRATION: *3622 Y 69 during 1950s*
BODYWORK: *Vertical grille; marine blue paint*
LAST KNOWN OWNER: *Roland Poncet (France)*

6. T26 GS No. 110 122
DELIVERY: *April 1950*
BODYWORK: *Vertical grille*
HISTORY: *Restored by Graber in 1980s*

FERRARI 212 EXPORT

The makings of a range

At the 1950 Paris Motor Show Ferrari announced its manufacturing programme for the next year. Alongside the 166 Inter and the 340 America the catalogues spoke of a 212 Export – although no such car was on display.

The new model used the short chassis of the 166 MM (wheelbase 2.25m) but was powered by a fresh version of the V12 engine designed by Gioacchino Colombo, bored out to a capacity of 2.5 litres. The first 212 Exports were completed at the beginning of 1951, in time to have their debut in the classic Italian road-races, the Tour of Sicily and April's Mille Miglia. At the same time the 212 Inter was unveiled, at the Turin Motor Show in April. Following on from the 166 Inter and the 195 Inter, the 212 Inter was a road car which had the same engine as the 212 Export but was built on a 2.60m wheelbase better suited to touring coachwork.

This apparently straightforward differentiation between the Inter and the Export does however have to be qualified, because there were plenty of half-breeds that make such a distinction more theoretical than real. On the short chassis of the 212 Export, coachbuilders Touring and Vignale were the most active. The former followed the delicious theme developed on the 166 MM, in Le Mans coupé form and as an open barchetta, and in all bodied a dozen cars. Vignale, meanwhile, out-did Touring by bodying at least 16 Exports in a style that was very much its own, and was the work of Giovanni Michelotti. His aggressive coupés, of which nine were made, have more to recommend themselves than his cabriolets, however. Other second-rank coachbuilders, such as Motto or Fontana, were also responsible for a few cars.

▶ *This Le Mans Berlinetta by Carrozzeria Touring (chassis 0112E) left the factory in May 1951. It was delivered to the Marquis Gerino Gerini, who drove it in the 1953 Mille Miglia.*

UNTIL THE 1950S PRODUCTION AT MARANELLO WAS ESSENTIALLY COMPETITION-ORIENTATED, WITH THE 212 INTER AND 212 EXPORT, FERRARI STARTED TO SKETCH OUT A MORE RATIONAL RANGE.

FERRARI 212 EXPORT 1951 • 1952

▲ *The first Tour de France, in 1951, was won by a 212 Export (chassis 0078E) bodied by Touring, a barchetta ineptly transformed into a convertible and sporting an ungainly hood.*

▼ *The 212 Export of Sterzi/Rovelli, typical of Vignale's berlinetta style, in the 1952 Mille Miglia.*

▲ *This Vignale coupé (chassis 0211EL) was delivered to Giovanni Agnelli, future boss of Fiat, in March 1952.*

With the 212 Export, Ferrari began to give his range a certain structure, offering customers a versatile model usable on the open road and yet nevertheless suitable for competition use at little cost. The results proved him right. Piero Scotti was Italian champion in the 'Sport' class with his Motto-bodied barchetta (chassis 094E), while Frenchmen Pagnibon and Barraquet won the first Tour de France, in 1951, with a Touring barchetta (0078E) disguised as a cabriolet by the addition of bumpers, a windscreen, and a hood.

Between concours d'élégance and endurance sporting events, the 212 Export was unbeatable.

TECHNICAL SPECIFICATION

CONFIGURATION	FRONT ENGINE; RWD
STRUCTURE	TUBULAR CHASSIS
BODY MATERIAL	STEEL
ENGINE	V12 (60 DEG)
VALVEGEAR	SINGLE OVERHEAD CAMSHAFT PER BANK
CAPACITY	2,562CC (68MM X 58.8MM)
POWER	150BHP AT 6,500RPM
FUEL SYSTEM	3 TWIN-CHOKE WEBER 32 DCF OR 136 DCF
GEARBOX	4-SPEED
WHEELBASE & TRACK	225CM; 127CM/125CM
WEIGHT	800KG APPROX
MAXIMUM SPEED	120MPH (200KPH)
NUMBER BUILT	33
CHASSIS NUMBERS	IN THE SEQUENCE 070E TO 0216E

MASERATI SPORT 2000
BERLINETTA

A beauty to excess

Competition cars always offer an ideal basis for developing a fast road-going GT – or so the theory goes. Thus Pinin Farina was tempted to tame the Maserati Sport 2000 (the A6 GCS) by transforming it into something more urbane. The short wheelbase, the big wheels and the long bonnet hiding a straight-six engine seemed to offer the perfect starting-point. All that remained was for the talent of Pinin Farina to give a form to this dream, working with stylist Aldo Brovarone, born in 1926 and working for the Turin design house since 1953. The reclothing of the A6 GSC barchetta, originally by Medardo Fantuzzi, was one of Brovarone's first jobs for Farina. The young stylist gave his talents free rein, exaggerating the proportions of the car, sketching a minimalist glasshouse compressed into a taut, simply-lined infrastructure, the whole sunk between muscular wings which were like the haunches of a cat. The mouth – the word is appropriate – was a superb oval grille, a prow whose vertical slats were like concave fangs. Hugging the tarmac, this aggressive gobbling snout seemed as if it were an escapee from a Grand Prix car.

▶ *This low-roofline berlinetta, originally found on chassis 2057 in 1954, was recreated by Pininfarina in the 1990s on chassis 2070.*

TECHNICAL SPECIFICATION	
CONFIGURATION	FRONT ENGINE; RWD
STRUCTURE	TUBULAR CHASSIS
BODY MATERIAL	STEEL
ENGINE	6-CYLINDER IN-LINE
VALVEGEAR	TWIN OVERHEAD CAMSHAFT
CAPACITY	1,985CC (76.5MM X 72MM)
POWER	170BHP AT 7,300RPM
FUEL SYSTEM	3 TWIN-CHOKE WEBER 40 DCO
GEARBOX	4-SPEED
WHEELBASE & TRACK	231CM; 133.5CM/122CM
LENGTH/WIDTH	384CM/153CM
WEIGHT	750KG
TYRES	6.00 X 16IN
MAXIMUM SPEED	143MPH (230KPH)
NUMBER BUILT	4 OUT OF A TOTAL OF 51 A6 GCS
CHASSIS NUMBERS	2041 TO 2098

It is difficult to resist the temptation of taking a hard-nosed racer and transforming it into a grand-touring road car. But with the Maserati Sport 2000 the idea ought to have stayed on the drawing board.

MASERATI SPORT 2000 BERLINETTA 1953 • 1954

▶ *The original '2057', at its first appearance, at the 1954 Turin Motor Show.*

◀ *Car number 2059 was shown at the 1954 Paris salon before being sold to a Florence-based racing driver.*

Alas, beyond its aesthetic success the Maserati A6 GCS was not a pleasant machine in this guise: it was as awkward to use as it was beautiful to contemplate. The problem was that it was prone to becoming unbearably hot during a race, and every bit as uncomfortable on the road. This led to the in-depth modification of two of the four berlinettas built, the cars being given an open body that was more spartan but better ventilated. The glorious closed coachwork was thus sacrificed on the altar of practicality. But the artistic attractions of this ultra-rare machine have since prompted the reconstruction of these two berlinettas in their original form.

▲ *Chassis 2060 has re-found its original identity, its closed coachwork having been recreated in 2002, in time for the 2003 Villa d'Este concours.*

THE FOUR MASERATI SPORT 2000 BERLINETTAS BODIED BY PININ FARINA

1. A6 GCS/2056
DELIVERY: *December 1953*
BODYWORK: *Red; restored by Campana in 1994*
FIRST OWNER: *Paolo Gravina di Catina (via Guglielmo Dei)*
HISTORY: *Giro di Sicilia, 1953*
LAST KNOWN OWNER: *Umberto Panini (Italy)*

2. A6 GCS/2057
DELIVERY: *January 1954*
BODYWORK: *Sky blue and mid blue; shallow glasshouse. Rebodied as a barchetta; original body put on chassis 2070*
FIRST OWNER: *Piero Palmieri (Rome)*
HISTORY: *Turin show, 1954; Louis Vuitton Classic, 1999*
LAST KNOWN OWNER: *Franco Lombardi (Italy)*

3. A6 GCS/2059
DELIVERY: *September 1954*
BODYWORK: *Red with white stripe; bonnet air scoop*
FIRST OWNER: *Alberto Magi Diligenti (Florence)*
HISTORY: *Paris show, 1954; Mille Miglia, 1955*
LAST KNOWN OWNER: *Italian collector*

4. A6 GCS/2060
DELIVERY: *September 1954*
BODYWORK: *Red with blue stripe. Rebodied as a barchetta; original body put on chassis 2089. Recently given new berlinetta body, in silver-grey*
FIRST OWNER: *Guglielmo Dei (Rome)*
HISTORY: *Villa d'Este, 2003*
LAST KNOWN OWNER: *Egon Zweimüller (Austria)*

1954 ■ 1956

FERRARI 375 MM

Sublime diversions

For its racing customers Ferrari developed a new model for the 1954 season: the 375 MM. It had a 4½-litre engine which despite its similar capacity was quite different from that of the Formula 1 cars: in fact this new engine, the Tipo 102, was an overbored 340 MM unit. For the new 375 MM chassis, Pinin Farina came up with two types of body: a berlinetta *competizione* and a spider *competizione*.

The first berlinetta (chassis 0358/AM) made its debut in the November 1953 Carrera Panamericana Mexico. The spider, meanwhile, had its baptism a few weeks later, in the 12 Heures de Casablanca in December 1953. This differentiation of the two models wasn't lost on those who appreciated such subtleties.

The 375 MM only needed a few modifications to be usable on the road. Accordingly a few berlinettas and open racers were converted for a civilian life while retaining their original Pinin Farina body. Others had special coachwork – by Pinin Farina, naturally enough, or by Scaglietti or Ghia.

▶ *The Berlinetta Aerodinamica Speciale (chassis 0456/AM) was one of the stars of the 1992 Bagatelle concours. It was built for Ingrid Bergman.*

TECHNICAL SPECIFICATION	
CONFIGURATION	FRONT ENGINE; RWD
STRUCTURE	TUBULAR CHASSIS
BODY MATERIAL	STEEL
ENGINE	V12 (60 DEG)
VALVEGEAR	SINGLE OVERHEAD CAMSHAFT PER BANK
CAPACITY	4,522CC (84MM X 68MM)
POWER	340BHP AT 7,000RPM
FUEL SYSTEM	3 TWIN-CHOKE WEBER
GEARBOX	4-SPEED
WHEELBASE & TRACK	260CM; 132.5CM/132CM
WEIGHT	900KG
TYRES	6.00 X 16IN FRONT; 7.50 X 16IN REAR
MAXIMUM SPEED	168MPH (270KPH)
NUMBER BUILT	24 OF ALL TYPES

At the dawn of the 1950s the distinction between road and track remained vague as far as Ferrari was concerned. It was thus no surprise that certain 'gentleman drivers' were tempted to make a road car of the delectable 375 MM.

▶ *Coachbuilder Scaglietti put this closed body on chassis 0402/AM, which had begun life as an open barchetta.*

▲ *A spider* competizione *(chassis 0450/AM) luxurously fitted-out for the former emperor of Vietnam.*

THE ROAD-GOING 375 MMs

THE PININ FARINA SPIDER COMPETIZIONE

Pinin Farina built 15 examples of the spider *competizione* for the 1954 season. Certain were equipped for a more touring use. This was most notably the case for chassis 0450/AM, which was sold to Bao Dai, the emperor of Vietnam from 1932 until 1945. Registered 06 IT 10, the car was finished in metallic blue with red upholstery. There was also a superb yellow spider (chassis number unknown), which appeared in a period advertisement. It had a small wraparound screen and overriders either side of the grille.

THE PININ FARINA BERLINETTA COMPETIZIONE

Pinin Farina built six roughly identical berlinettas. Chassis 0358/AM, 0368/AM and 0380/AM were to racing specification, but the other three cars had a presentation more suited to road use, in particular having bumpers front and rear.

- 0378/AM. Acquired in January 1954 by Enrico Wax of Genoa, and registered 73400 GE, this was painted metallic blue and had imitation-leather upholstery. There was a front bumper, the rear lights were protruding, and there was chrome trim on the sills, the screen surround and around the headlamps.
- 0416/AM. This cream-coloured car stood out on account of its winding windows, bumperettes, opening boot, chrome window frames, protruding rear lights and its right-hand seat which could be slid sideways. The car survives in Switzerland.
- 0472/AM. This two-tone car (blue body with black roof; beige interior), delivered to Alfredo Ducato in California, in November 1954, had front and rear bumpers as on 0378/AM, but didn't have that car's more pronounced wings.

THE PININ FARINA BERLINETTA AERODINAMICA SPECIALE (No. 0456/AM)

This one-off berlinetta was built by Pinin Farina for the 1954 Paris Motor Show.

▼ *The Coupé Speciale (chassis 0490/AM) created by Pinin Farina for the 1955 Turin Motor Show.*

◀ *The cabriolet built in 1954 for the King of Belgium counts as one of the masterpieces of Italian coachwork.*

The rear, with its recessed window and its wings topped by slender flying buttresess, heralded a new style which would be found on other Pinin Farina prototypes and ultimately on the Dino 206 GT. The front was made more sleek, meanwhile, by the adoption of retractable headlamps, and the sides featured a deep elliptical scallop. This stylistically important creation was ordered by Ingrid Bergman, but the Swedish actress never took delivery. The car, today the property of the Gollomb Family Trust, of Springfield, Illinois, was shown at the Bagatelle Automobiles Classiques concours in 1992 and at Pebble Beach in 1994.

THE PININ FARINA CABRIOLET SPECIALE (No. 0488/AM)

Constructed in December 1954 for King Leopold of Belgium, this was one of Pinin Farina's masterpieces. The ivory-upholstered black body sat on a special chassis powered by a 375 Plus engine, and the strongly classical but perfectly proportioned lines prefigured those of the 250 GT California. Since 1969 this gem of a car has been part of the Wayne Collomb collection in Chicago.

THE PININ FARINA COUPÉ COMPETIZIONE (No. 0490/AM)

Shown at the 1955 Turin *salon*, this car was bought by Inico Bernabei. It differed from the 'regular' 375 MM berlinettas by having the finned rear wings and oval grille that would later be taken up on various 250 GTs.

THE GHIA COUPE SPECIALE (No. 0476/AM)

One of the rare Ferraris that escaped the clutches of Pinin Farina. Was that a good thing? Clothed in pink and grey paint, this coupé built by Ghia for Ralph Wilkie was hardly a creature of beauty: the sharp rear wings, two-tone paint and excessive chrome were too much of a concession to American tastes. Displayed at the 1955 Turin show, the car spent its life in the States, until it was sold at the Bonhams auction in Gstaad in December 2002.

THE SCAGLIETTI BERLINETTA SPECIALE (No. 0402/AM)

Originally a spider *competizione* built in 1954, this chassis received a new body by Scaglietti in 1956. Seemingly influenced by the Mercedes 300SL, this unique vehicle was built for film director Roberto Rossellini. Seen at the 1998 Bagatelle concours, the car survives in all its splendour in the US, in the Jon Shirley collection.

1957

JAGUAR XK-SS

An opportune conversion

From the track to the road, from the D-type to the XK-SS: the nuances are subtle. Despite its victories at Le Mans in 1955 and 1956, the Jaguar D-type was no longer pulling in the customers. It had been made in respectable numbers – 59 in all, if you combine works cars and those sold to privateers. But what that meant was that all the teams who were interested in the 'D' had already bought them, while the rest were casting their eyes more towards Ferrari, Maserati or Aston Martin. So what could Jaguar do with the unsold cars?

The solution was to convert the D-type into a road car, so that Jaguar could amortise the costs of the monocoques that were still lying about. The XK-SS was thus distinguished from the D-type only by the various modifications necessary for it to take to the open road. A proper windscreen with a substantial frame replaced the simple curved aeroscreen of the racing cars, while a tightly-drawn hood and fixed side-windows gave some protection from the elements – the fitting of a hood requiring the suppression of the tailfin and its integral headrest. Slim chrome bumpers added a civilised touch, as did the leather upholstery and the chrome on the headlamp cowls and the rear light plinths. Finally, there was a small luggage-rack on the tail, a chrome guard for the silencer, and some badging on the bonnet.

▶ The windscreen, bumpers, side windows and hood are the only accessories that distinguish an XK-SS from a D-type.

TECHNICAL SPECIFICATION	
CONFIGURATION	FRONT ENGINE; RWD
STRUCTURE	MONOCOQUE WITH SQUARE-TUBE FRONT SUBFRAME
BODY MATERIAL	STEEL
ENGINE	6-CYLINDER IN-LINE
VALVEGEAR	DOUBLE OVERHEAD-CAMSHAFT
CAPACITY	3,442CC (83MM X 106MM)
POWER	250BHP AT 5,800RPM
FUEL SYSTEM	3 TWIN-CHOKE WEBER 45 DCOE
GEARBOX	4-SPEED
WHEELBASE & TRACK	229CM; 127CM/122CM
LENGTH/WIDTH/HEIGHT	391CM/165CM/81CM
WEIGHT	901KG
TYRES	6.50 X 16IN
MAXIMUM SPEED	158MPH (254KPH)
NUMBER BUILT	18

But in its essentials the XK-SS remained true to the superb D-type, of which it retained the lithe sensual lines laid down by aerodynamicist Malcolm Sayer. You thus found the same beautiful centre-lock wheels, for example, as well as details such as the fuel filler in the cockpit – characteristics that attested to the sporting origins of the XK-SS. The entire front end, taking in the wings, bonnet and lights, tipped forward to give access to the engine

. . . Or how Jaguar discovered the art of making use of the left-overs. When the D-Type, a several-times winner at Le Mans, was no longer attracting buyers, Jaguar decided to convert it for road use.

room, where the dry-sump power unit was no different from that of the D-type.

Production began in January 1957, but a few weeks later catastrophe struck. The Jaguar factory at Browns Lane was ravaged by a fire. Several hundred cars were destroyed and production was stopped for six weeks. Manufacture of the XK-SS was not restarted. It had only lasted for a month and a half, between January and February 1957, limiting output to only 16 precious cars. To this can be added two further examples, created later by the factory from existing D-types. Among the lucky few who took the wheel of an XK-SS was film star Steve McQueen, a great lover of racing cars.

A victim of the twists of fate, the XK-SS went on to become one of the most sought-after of Jaguars.

1959 ■ 1962

FERRARI 250 GT
BERLINETTA

Classicism at its peak

There is no shortage of true classics in Ferrari's history. Their fame derives either from their sporting successes or from their looks, moulded out of the long and faithful collaboration between Ferrari and the Pinin Farina styling house. But in the prolific 250 GT family there is one model that stands out, because it illustrates so marvellously that wonderful notion of Gran Turismo invented by Italian car-makers. A thoroughbred among thoroughbreds, the 250 GT Berlinetta was born to race, before being made available to a handful of aesthetes keen to offer themselves a slice of the ostentatious high-life.

Going back a little, the first prototypes of a sporting version of the 250 GT had appeared in 1955. The initiative came naturally enough from Pinin Farina, who transposed the flowing lines of the 375 MM Berlinetta onto the mechanicals of the 250 GT. This was no mere caprice: it was a response to Enzo Ferrari's continual desire to explore the interplay between road and track. Thus a 250 GT *competizione* was offered to independent drivers from 1956. For each racing season the Scaglietti body shop produced a small series, to Pinin Farina's design: 9 in 1956, 23 in 1957, 30 in 1958, 10 in 1959. Each year the design was improved in detail, and the mechanicals uprated…and each year the car's competition record was boosted by numerous victories in the GT class.

In 1959 Pinin Farina completely revised his original, a new style, more fluid and more modern, being introduced in time for that year's Le Mans. Seven examples were made, but then, for the 1959 Paris show, Ferrari and Pinin Farina unveiled a new development of the Berlinetta: the lines were the same as those of the Le Mans cars, but the wheelbase was reduced by 20cm – roughly 8 inches. Those were 20 centimetres that changed everything, and saw the 250 GT Berlinetta enter the pantheon of Italian coachbuilding greats. The proportions were now perfect, giving the car a heady mix of grace and power.

▶ *It was* passo corto *for the Italians, and 'short wheelbase' or swb for the British – but whatever you call it, the 250 GT Berlinetta is an unchallenged masterpiece.*

The '250 GT' name covers a whole family of grand-touring cars that have become legends. At the top of the tree is the short-wheelbase 'Berlinetta'.

FERRARI 250 GT BERLINETTA 1959 • 1962

▲ *In city dress the 250 GT Berlinetta has bumpers, winding windows, and a steel body.*

TECHNICAL SPECIFICATION

CONFIGURATION	FRONT ENGINE; RWD
STRUCTURE	TUBULAR CHASSIS
BODY MATERIAL	STEEL
ENGINE	V12 (60 DEG)
VALVEGEAR	SINGLE OVERHEAD CAMSHAFT PER BANK
CAPACITY	2,953CC (78MM X 58.8MM)
POWER	240BHP AT 7,000RPM
FUEL SYSTEM	3 TWIN-CHOKE WEBER 40 DCN
GEARBOX	4-SPEED
WHEELBASE & TRACK	240CM; 135.4CM/135CM
LENGTH/WIDTH/HEIGHT	415CM/169CM/126CM
WEIGHT	1,160KG
TYRES	6.00 X 16IN
MAXIMUM SPEED	162MPH (260KPH)
NUMBER BUILT	87 LUSSO OUT OF A TOTAL OF 160 BERLINETTAS
CHASSIS NUMBERS (LUSSO)	IN THE SEQUENCE 1993 GT TO 4065 GT

Beyond its revised dimensions, giving rise to the 'short chassis' or 'short wheelbase' ('swb') tag, the new Tipo 539 chassis also benefited from disc brakes. The 250 GT Berlinetta was above all intended for competition, as with preceding generations of 250 GT, and it covered itself in glory, not least in winning the Tour de France three times in a row, in 1960, 1961 and 1962.

In response to demand, Ferrari didn't delay in offering road-going versions called *Lusso* – as opposed to the much more spartan *competizione* model. The engine was less highly-tuned, making do with 240bhp instead of 280bhp, and Scaglietti made the body in steel rather than in aluminium, with front and rear bumpers, and with the more plush interior equipped with winding windows and quarter-lights.

Once again, Enzo Ferrari could offer his demanding customers a machine forged on the race-track.

▼ *The first cars, produced in 1959 and 1960 can be recognised by the less taut lines of the side windows.*

1960

ALFA ROMEO 3500 SUPERSPORT

Multiple curtain-call

As with so many farewells, that of Alfa Romeo to its sporting public, at the end of 1951, was purely temporary – the demon of motor-racing couldn't be chased away that easily. Not only that, but a new World Championship was on the horizon for 1953. With this in mind, engineer Gioacchino Colombo drew up a six-cylinder barchetta. On 25 October 1952, at Monza, the new car had its official launch; it was called *Disco Volante*, or 'flying saucer', on account of its fantastic elliptical bodywork dreamt up by coach-builder Touring.

Stunning though it was, this futuristic machine was not up to scratch on the track, and after disappointing trials wasn't allowed the chance of being used in anger. For 1953 a new model was developed, called the 6C 3000 CM and differing both in its running gear (it had a de Dion back axle) and in its more conventional Colli-designed body. The new Alfa Romeo had its debut in the 1953 Mille Miglia and against all expectations dominated the first hours of the race, with Juan Manuel Fangio, despite various problems, managing to hold on to second place. A few weeks later, at Le Mans, Alfa Romeo failed to repeat this exploit, all three cars retiring – a set-back that saw the company abandon the rest of the racing season.

In all, eight 6C 3000 CM chassis had been laid down, and two of these were reconditioned for road-going use. Chassis 0126, one of the 1953 Le Mans cars, was two years later given an attractive body by Boano, for President of Argentina Juan Peron. Another berlinetta, chassis 0128, was stripped down in 1954 and passed to Pinin Farina, his version of the car duly appearing at the April 1956 Turin show as the Superflow. For a coachbuilder, a competition chassis has always offered a stimulating starting-point, and Pinin Farina rose to the occasion with boldness: the car had cowled headlamps, a concave side moulding, and a full-glazed cockpit cover with a panoramic windscreen.

Six months later the Superflow reappeared at the Paris show under the name Superflow II. It had changed colour, swapping its white coachwork with a blue stripe for a colour scheme of red with white detailing. The car was then seen at

▶ *The final development of Alfa Romeo 6C 3000 CM chassis 0128, the 3500 Supersport coupé has come to rest in the Rosso Bianco collection.*

THE ALFA ROMEO 6C 3000 CM, THE CAR THAT GAVE BIRTH TO THE 3500 SUPERSPORT, HAD A SPORTING CAREER THAT WAS NEITHER LONG NOR BRILLIANT. TO LESSEN THE DISAPPOINTMENT OF THE CAR'S CREATORS, PININ FARINA GAVE THE ILL-FATED CAR A CHANCE TO BOUNCE BACK – SEVERAL TIMES OVER.

ALFA ROMEO 3500 SUPERSPORT 1960

The 3500 Supersport anticipated the general lines of the Alfa Romeo Giulia Spider Duetto.

▲ *Pinin Farina was not immune to aeronautical influences, as the cockpit cover and tailfins of the Superflow testify.*

the 1959 Geneva *salon*, converted into the Spyder Super Sport, with a boat tail that prefigured the design of the 1966 Alfa Romeo Giulia Spider Duetto. A year later, at the 1960 Geneva show, Pinin Farina displayed the final metamorphosis of '0128': the cockpit was again enclosed by an all-glass top, but this time the windscreen was not panoramic.

This 3500 Supersport ended up in the superb Rosso Bianco collection in Germany, the perfect setting for such a jewel.

TECHNICAL SPECIFICATION

CONFIGURATION	FRONT ENGINE; RWD
STRUCTURE	TUBULAR CHASSIS
BODY MATERIAL	STEEL
ENGINE	6-CYLINDER IN-LINE
VALVEGEAR	DOUBLE OVERHEAD-CAMSHAFT
CAPACITY	3,495CC (87MM X 98MM)
POWER	275BHP AT 6,500RPM
FUEL SYSTEM	6 HORIZONTAL CARBURETTORS
GEARBOX	5-SPEED
WHEELBASE & TRACK	225CM; 131CM FRONT AND REAR
WEIGHT	980KG
TYRES	6.50 X 16IN
MAXIMUM SPEED	150MPH (240KPH)
NUMBER BUILT	8 (6C 3000 CM)
CHASSIS NUMBERS	0121 TO 0128

1960 ■ 1962

ASTON MARTIN DB 4 GT
ZAGATO

The Anglo-Italian alliance

Aston Martin entered a new era with the October 1958 launch of the DB4. After a series of superb sports cars which were elegant and eminently British, Aston decided to move away from its home-grown style by bringing in some Italian expertise. The idea was then fashionable in England, with BMC having called in Pinin Farina, while Triumph had turned to Giovanni Michelotti.

The Aston Martin DB4 was intended to serve as the platform for a new racing programme. The first move was the DB4 GT of October 1959, a shortened, lightened and smoothed-out version that still wore the Superleggera Touring signature. The second move came at the 1960 London Motor Show, when Aston Martin unveiled a spectacular evolution of the DB4 GT.

On the body sides there was a small 'Z' in chrome, a Z' that signified 'Zagato': it was the famed Italian coachbuilder and his stylist Ercole Spada who had created this truly original body on the GT's shortened wheelbase, and the DB4 GT Zagato

▶ *One of the most beautiful alchemies in the history of the motor car, the improbable alliance of Zagato style and Aston Martin mechanicals gave birth to the magnificent DB4 GT Zagato (here one of the 1989 'Sanction II' replicas).*

TECHNICAL SPECIFICATION	
CONFIGURATION	FRONT ENGINE; RWD
STRUCTURE	PLATFORM CHASSIS WITH TUBULAR BODY FRAME
BODY MATERIAL	ALUMINIUM
ENGINE	6-CYLINDER IN-LINE
VALVEGEAR	DOUBLE OVERHEAD-CAMSHAFT
CAPACITY	3,670CC (92MM X 92MM)
POWER	314BHP AT 6,000RPM
FUEL SYSTEM	3 TWIN-CHOKE WEBER 45 DCOE
GEARBOX	4-SPEED (DBS 432)
WHEELBASE & TRACK	236.2CM; 137.2CM/135.9CM
LENGTH/WIDTH/HEIGHT	426.7CM/165.7CM/127CM
WEIGHT	1,171KG
TYRES	6.00 X 16IN
MAXIMUM SPEED	154MPH (247KPH)
NUMBER BUILT	19 WITH ZAGATO COACHWORK; 2 AS DP 215; 4 'SANCTION II' AND ONE WITH BERTONE COACHWORK
CHASSIS NUMBERS	IN THE SEQUENCE 0176 TO 0201

Aston Martin made its entry into the 'GT' class with a coupé that was desirable as much for its beauty as for its rarity. This time Aston's Italian partner was coachbuilder Zagato.

ASTON MARTIN DB 4 GT ZAGATO 1960 • 1962

▲ *This 'lowline' DB4 GT Zagato (car 0193/R) started its life in France.*

▼ *The famous '2 VEV' (car 013/R) was campaigned by Essex Racing Stables.*

was to be be an object of unabashed admiration, on account of the harmony of its lines, unsullied by any superfluous decoration. The volumes were deftly judged and sculpted with subtlety, the stylist showing his command of the art with his mastery of the curved surfaces, while the traditional shape of the grille was treated with sensuality and elegance.

The production run of fewer than 20 cars all differed one from the other in their details, such as the shaping of the grille, the positioning and shape of the air vents on the bonnet and body sides, the indicators, the width of the wheelarches, and sometimes even the height of the glasshouse. Here's a closer look at these 19 very special motor cars…

THE 19 ASTON MARTIN DB 4 GT ZAGATOS

1. 0176/R
DELIVERY: *July 1961*
REGISTRATION: *BMN 4 then AE 500 (GB)*
BODYWORK: *Red*
FIRST OWNER: *Jaime Ortiz-Patiño*
HISTORY: *Geneva Motor Show, 1961*
LAST KNOWN OWNER: *Hubert Fabri (France)*

2. 0177/R
DELIVERY: *December 1961*
REGISTRATION: *EP 151 then 6 ECE*
BODYWORK: *Metallic blue*
FIRST OWNER: *Lord Portman*
LAST KNOWN OWNER: *Car GB domiciled*

3. 0178/L
DELIVERY: *March 1961*
REGISTRATION: *AG-34255 (Switzerland)*
BODYWORK: *Red; widened rear arches*
FIRST OWNER: *Fridolin Haechler (Switzerland)*
HISTORY: *Spa GP, 1961*
LAST KNOWN OWNER: *Jerry Rosenstock (California)*

4. 0179/L
DELIVERY: *February 1961*
REGISTRATION: *XV 71*
BODYWORK: *Silver-grey with black interior*
FIRST OWNER: *Archie Bryde (Italy)*

5. 0180/L
DELIVERY: *February 1961*
REGISTRATION: *VD-777Z (Switzerland)*
BODYWORK: *White*
FIRST OWNER: *Jean Kerguen (Casablanca)*
HISTORY: *Le Mans, 1961 (car No.1)*
LAST KNOWN OWNER: *William Loughran*

6. 0181/L
DELIVERY: *March 1961*
REGISTRATION: *FI 299852 (Italy) then SUA 50 (GB)*
BODYWORK: *Metallic green; bonnet vent*
FIRST OWNER: *Elio Zagato*
LAST KNOWN OWNER: *Richard Williams (GB)*

7. 0182/R
DELIVERY: *June 1961*
REGISTRATION: *1 VEV (GB)*
BODYWORK: *Metallic green; widened rear wings*
FIRST OWNER: *Essex Racing Stables*
HISTORY: *Le Mans 1961 (car No. 2)*
LAST KNOWN OWNER: *William Loughran*

8. 0183/R
DELIVERY: *June 1961*
REGISTRATION: *2 VEV (GB)*
BODYWORK: *Metallic green; widened rear arches; then converted to DP209, July 1962*
FIRST OWNER: *Essex Racing Stables*
HISTORY: *Le Mans, 1961*
LAST KNOWN OWNERS: *David and Toni Eyles*

9. 0184/R
DELIVERY: *October 1961*
REGISTRATION: *4359 ML then 8 DBL (GB)*
BODYWORK: *Metallic green*
FIRST OWNER: *Dunlop*
HISTORY: Autocar, *April 1962*
LAST KNOWN OWNER: *In Germany (Poulain Le Fur auction, December 1990)*

10. 0185/R
DELIVERY: *June 1962*
REGISTRATION: *XNE 1 (GB)*
BODYWORK: *Metallic green*
FIRST OWNER: *N. Morton (GB)*
LAST KNOWN OWNER: *William Loughran*

11. 0186/R
DELIVERY: *December 1961*
REGISTRATION: *315 (Australia)*
BODYWORK: *White with red interior; then metallic pale green*
FIRST OWNER: *Laurie O'Neill (Australia)*
LAST KNOWN OWNER: *John Goldsmith (GB)*

12. 0187/R
DELIVERY: *October 1961*
REGISTRATION: *NA-451710 (Italy)*
BODYWORK: *Blue; bumpers; bonnet vent*
FIRST OWNER: *Ugo Sorrentino (Rome)*
HISTORY: *Turin Motor Show, 1961*
LAST KNOWN OWNER: *Nick Begovich (California)*

13. 0188/L
DELIVERY: *October 1961*
REGISTRATION: *251146 PD (Italy) then 29 ALY (GB)*
BODYWORK: *Silver-grey with grey interior; forward-mounted headlamps*
FIRST OWNER: *Antonio Mochetti (Milan)*
LAST KNOWN OWNER: *Philip Jones (GB)*

14. 0189/R
DELIVERY: *December 1962*
REGISTRATION: *37 PH (GB)*
BODYWORK: *Blue-grey*
FIRST OWNER: *Mike Harting (GB)*
LAST KNOWN OWNER: *Herb Wildholzs (NL)*

15. 0190/L
DELIVERY: *June 1962*
REGISTRATION: *MA 4160 (Sweden) then AUJ 6551 (GB)*
BODYWORK: *Grey; broader grille mesh*
FIRST OWNER: *James Murray (Paris)*
LAST KNOWN OWNER: *Les Edgar*

16. 0191/R
DELIVERY: *June 1961*
REGISTRATION: *63 PH (GB)*
BODYWORK: *'Lowline' DP 209; grey, then pale green*
FIRST OWNER: *John Coombs*
HISTORY: *Brands Hatch, May 1962*
LAST KNOWN OWNER: *Les Maybury*

17. 0193/R
DELIVERY: *June 1962*
REGISTRATION: *475 TTA 75 (France) then 6003 ND (GB)*
BODYWORK: *'Lowline' DP 209; sky blue; now dark green*
FIRST OWNER: *Jean Kerguen*
HISTORY: *Le Mans, 1962 (No. 12) and 1963 (No. 19)*
LAST KNOWN SITUATION: *Sold by Lukas Hüni*

18. 0199/L
DELIVERY: *December 1960*
REGISTRATION: *VMS 10 (GB)*
BODYWORK: *Metallic green with black then red interior*
FIRST OWNER: *Aeronautica*
LAST KNOWN OWNER: *Bob Stockman (US)*

19. 0200/R
DELIVERY: *September 1960*
REGISTRATION: *22 XKX (GB)*
BODYWORK: *Dark green with chrome side strip*
FIRST OWNERS: *Dick Wilkins / Rob Walker (GB)*
HISTORY: *London Motor Show, 1960 (Zagato stand); Le Mans, 1962 (No.14)*
LAST KNOWN OWNER: *Simon Draper*

To the 19 DB4 GT Zagatos should be added three other special bodies:

- *The two DP215s bodied in the same style as the DB 212: 0194/R, which ran at Le Mans in 1963 (No. 7) and 1964 (No. 18), and 0195/R which ran at Le Mans in 1963 (No. 8).*
- *The Jet coupé built by Bertone on chassis 0201/L and displayed at the Geneva and Turin motor shows in 1961.*

Finally, Aston Martin made four replicas in 1989; they were called 'Sanction II' and carried the numbers 0192/R, 0196/R, 0197/R and 0198/R.

1962 ■ 1964

PANHARD CD

The glory of aerodynamics

The Deutsch & Bonnet firm, which had upheld the hopes of France in motor sport during the previous decade, imploded in 1962, when the two people behind the small enterprise separated. René Bonnet went his own way, turning to Renault for his engines, before being taken over by Matra. Charles Deutsch, meanwhile, created the engineering consultancy SECA-CD (latterly SERA-CD), and remained faithful to Panhard, who had been DB's partner for many years.

The two men found themselves face-to-face at 1962's Le Mans. René Bonnet fielded his Renault-engined Djet while Charles Deutsch linked his name with that of Panhard on the sides of the Panhard CD. The car's baptism was a resounding success, the car driven by Alain Bertaud and André Guilhaudin winning the Index of Performance. Four months later, Panhard unveiled a road version of the CD at the October motor show in Paris.

Power came from the Tigre version of the new 848cc 'M6' flat-twin used on all the 1963 range – whereas the four prototypes for Le Mans had used a 702cc engine. As for the chassis, that had a central backbone and transverse-leaf front suspension, making it a natural evolution of the previous DB mainstay, the HBR5 coupé. Where the CD stood apart was in its aerodynamic coachwork. As with all Charles Deutsch's work, in this instance in conjunction with aerodynamicist Lucien Romani, the body was meticulously shaped. The rounded lines were streamlined and carefully wrapped around the key 'hard points'. Thus the long tail tapered, enclosed the wheels, and finished in a miniature Kamm tail, while the roof was characterised by a discreet 'double bubble' shape. The aerodynamic coefficient

TECHNICAL SPECIFICATION

CONFIGURATION	FRONT ENGINE; FWD
STRUCTURE	STEEL BACKBONE FRAME
BODY MATERIAL	GLASS-FIBRE
ENGINE	2-CYLINDER HORIZONTALLY-OPPOSED, AIR-COOLED
VALVEGEAR	SINGLE CENTRAL CAMSHAFT
CAPACITY	848CC (84.8MM X 75MM)
POWER	50BHP AT 5,750RPM
FUEL SYSTEM	ZENITH 32 NDIX TWIN-CHOKE; TWIN CARBS ON RALLYE
GEARBOX	4-SPEED
WHEELBASE & TRACK	225CM; 120CM/110CM
LENGTH/WIDTH/HEIGHT	400CM/160CM/118.5CM
WEIGHT	580KG
TYRES	145 X 380
MAXIMUM SPEED	99MPH (160KPH) STANDARD 112MPH (180KPH) RALLYE
NUMBER BUILT	4 PROTOTYPES AND 159 PRODUCTION CARS
CHASSIS NUMBERS	101 TO 104 (PROTOTYPES) 105 TO 284 (PRODUCTION)

THEY CALLED PANHARD THE DOYEN OF FRENCH MAKES, AND RIGHT TO THE END THE PIONEER FRENCH FIRM SHOWED ITS SENSE OF CREATIVITY. THE CD WAS ONE OF ITS LAST FLOURISHES.

was 0.22 on the production car, a figure which was quite remarkable – even though the Le Mans prototypes had managed a figure of 0.17.

Homologation for the French market was secured in February 1963 but a pre-series of 25 cars was built before the 1962 Paris show, assembly being looked after by the Chappe brothers at Brie-Comte-Robert. Subsequently production moved to Vélam at Suresnes.

From January 1964 a Rallye version was available, with twin carbs and a gearbox and final drive revised to profit from the increased performance. But the Panhard CD was too idiosyncratic, and sold poorly, with the result that production was stopped in July 1965. Two years later, Panhard was dead, sacrificed by Citroën, who had finally fully absorbed the company in April 1965.

▲ *The beehive hair-do of the driver is more dated than the Panhard CD's aerodynamic lines.*

1963 JAGUAR D-TYPE COUPÉ

Resurrection

He always had a bit of a taciturn look about him, Giovanni Michelotti, when you crossed his path at a motor show, at Geneva or Turin. And yet behind that modest façade hid without a doubt one of the most original talents of the fifties and sixties. Whatever, he was certainly the most prolific stylist of his generation. His creations for the big manufacturers and for the Turinese coachbuilders are pretty much innumerable, but from time to time he also built prototypes in his own workshops.

Such is the case with the very special D-type that was shown at the 1963 Geneva *salon*. It had been built in Turin on the remains of car XKD-513, which had run at Le Mans in 1957 and 1958 in the French Blue of the Peignaux team. Registered 6478 AT 69, and lacking the characteristic D-type rear fin, the Jaguar finished third in 1957, behind the two Ecurie Ecosse D-types; the team consisted of Jean Lucas (future founder of French magazine *Sport Auto*) and Lyons industrialist Jean-Marie Brussin, racing under the pseudonym 'Mary'. The following year Brussin was paired with André Guelphi, part-time racing driver and future player in the Elf scandal, and better known in Marseilles as 'Dédé-la-Sardine'! In the seventh hour of the race, in pouring rain, 'Mary' lost control of the Jaguar, left the road at the Dunlop Curve, and was fatally injured. The car having turned over, the body wasn't too damaged, and Giovanni Michelotti bought the wreck to transform it into an elegant coupé.

The design recalled in some ways the same stylist's Triumph TR4, but the odd proportions of the chassis, with its big wheels, short wheelbase and long overhangs, resulted in a magnificent profile. Nothing in these crisp lines led one to suspect the origins of the car, which was to remain a one-off: Michelotti's

TECHNICAL SPECIFICATION

CONFIGURATION	FRONT ENGINE; RWD
STRUCTURE	MONOCOQUE WITH SQUARE-TUBE FRONT SUBFRAME
BODY MATERIAL	STEEL
ENGINE	6-CYLINDER IN-LINE
VALVEGEAR	DOUBLE OVERHEAD CAMSHAFT
CAPACITY	3,442CC (83MM X 106MM)
POWER	250BHP AT 5,800RPM
FUEL SYSTEM	3 TWIN-CHOKE WEBER 45 DCOE
GEARBOX	4-SPEED
WHEELBASE & TRACK	229CM; 127CM FRONT AND REAR
WEIGHT	1,200KG
TYRES	6.50 X 16IN
MAXIMUM SPEED	168MPH (270KPH)
NUMBER BUILT	1 (OUT OF 59 XKD MADE)
CHASSIS NUMBER	XKD-513

LONG AFTER THE DISAPPEARANCE OF THE XK-SS, THE IDEA OF CIVILISING THE FIRE-BREATHING D-TYPE RESURFACED. THIS TIME, THE MECHANICALS WERE UNRECOGNISABLE UNDER THE CAR'S NEW MICHELOTTI CLOTHES.

design made no reference to contemporary Jaguars or to the voluptuously aerodynamic lines so memorably defined by the talented Malcolm Sayer.

Under its graceful skin the Jaguar D-type coupé hid a truly thoroughbred set of mechanicals. The engine was the classic 'XK' unit, dry-sumped as on all D-types, and there were Dunlop disc brakes all-round, plus the usual torsion-bar suspension and rack-and-pinion steering.

Today Giovanni Michelotti's favourite car lives happily in a French collection.

▲ *D-type XKD-513 took on a new life at the 1963 Geneva salon, showcasing a new body created by Giovanni Michelotti.*

1963 • 1965

FERRARI 250 LM

Genetic modification

The notion of *grand tourisme* is eminently elastic. Feeling the threat of the Ford-powered Cobras, Ferrari decided on drastic action for the 1964 season. Glorious though the 250 GTO might have been, it was in the process, living myth or not, of becoming old-hat. Ferrari therefore decided to replace it with a car based on the 250P prototype.

And so the 250 LM (short for 'Le Mans') made its entrance at the 1963 Paris Motor Show. It was Ferrari's first mid-engined car, and was directly derived from the 250P which had appeared during the 1963 racing season: Pininfarina merely added a roof and a thicker rear hoop to transform the open prototype into a closed berlinetta.

In April 1964 Ferrari applied for homologation of the 250 LM in the GT class – suggesting that the car would eventually make it to series-production, but also in the hope of confusing its identity with that of the 250 GTO. Unsurprisingly, the FIA inspectors weren't that indulgent, especially as the homologation of the 250 GTO had already led to protests from certain rivals – and quite rightly, too, as the beautiful racer had been homologated somewhat dubiously on the back of the 250 GT.

▶ *A 250 LM still proudly bearing the insignia of Luigi Chinetti's North American Racing Team, or NART.*

TECHNICAL SPECIFICATION	
CONFIGURATION	MID-ENGINE; RWD
STRUCTURE	TUBULAR CHASSIS
BODY MATERIAL	STEEL
ENGINE	V12 (60 DEG)
VALVEGEAR	SINGLE OVERHEAD CAM PER BANK
CAPACITY	3,286CC (77MM X 58.8MM)
POWER	320BHP
FUEL SYSTEM	6 TWIN-CHOKE 38DCN WEBER CARBURETTORS
GEARBOX	5-SPEED
WHEELBASE & TRACK	240CM; 135CM/134CM
LENGTH/WIDTH/HEIGHT	409CM/170CM/111.5CM
WEIGHT	850KG
TYRES	FRONT 5.50 X 15IN; REAR 7.00 X 15IN
MAXIMUM SPEED	183MPH (295KPH)
NUMBER BUILT	32
CHASSIS NUMBERS	IN THE SEQUENCE 5149 TO 8165

It was supposed to replace the 250 GTO, but ended up as an ambiguous halfway-house between a racing prototype and a grand tourer. Rare indeed were the privileged few who had the chance to use a 250 LM on the road.

FERRARI 250 LM 1963 • 1965

▲ *There are plenty of similarities between the rear of the 250 LM and that of the contemporary 1964 GTO.*

In any case, production of the 250 LM would fetch up far below the the hundred examples required, as in the end only 32 cars were built. It would thus remain classed as a prototype, and Ferrari would have to continue with the GTO in the GT class, with a modernised body for the 1964 season.

On the 'production' 250 LMs there were certain modifications relative to chassis 5149, the Paris prototype. As far as the body was concerned, the air ducts on the rear wings were more pronounced and the glasshouse was extended and no longer included an integral aerofoil. The engine, meanwhile, was enlarged from 3 litres to 3.3 litres, pushing power up from 300bhp to 320bhp. Despite this, the 250 Le Mans appellation was retained, the name '275 LM' never being more than an informal and unofficial tag. In the course of its career many examples received a modified front, with sleeker lines and an enlarged oval air intake, these changes being the work of Piero Drogo, boss of Carrozzeria Sports Cars. The last of the 32 cars was delivered during 1965.

Before that, at the 1965 Geneva Motor Show, Pininfarina unveiled a roadgoing version of the 250 LM. Built on chassis 6025, the eighteenth made, it was distinguished by its more luxurious interior, with a more lavish dashboard and better upholstery, and by its overrider bumperettes, its curved rear screen and its two-part opening roof that made access easier. Painted white with blue stripes, this vehicle left for the US in 1971. Another road-going 250 LM (chassis 5995) was prepared for Count Volpi di Misurata, while in 1966 coachbuilder Scaglietti, who had built all the 250 LM bodies, carried out its own conversions, painted in silver-grey and given a huge panoramic plexiglas rear screen, air-conditioning, and magnesium-alloy wheels.

With these exceptions, the 250 LM led an exclusively sporting life, the most prestigious result being Jochen Rindt and Masten Gregory's 1965 Le Mans win with car 5893, entered by US Ferrari importer NART.

▼ *Pininfarina was responsible for this road-converted 250 LM, car number 6025.*

1966 – 1969

FORD GT 40

America enters the fray

The idea of spinning off a road-going derivative of the GT 40 germinated during 1965, and Ford's first street version emerged in January 1966, carrying chassis number 1013 and British registration OVX 355D. It had all the attributes of a grand tourer, right down to its metallic grey paintwork. Externally it could be identified by a few small details – the door handles, the chrome 'Ford' lettering on the bonnet, and the blue-oval badge on the sills. Inside, everything was conceived to erase the original's race-car spartanism, with British coachbuilder Harold Radford recruited to domesticate the cockpit. Accordingly the seats were in black leather, and there was carpet for the floor and the pannier fuel tanks, and pockets in the doors. The engine was also made more docile, with power reduced from 380bhp to 335bhp and a clutch and flywheel better suited to town driving; additionally the brakes were gentler to apply and the dampers softer. There was even the option of air-conditioning, for the truly faint of heart! In February 1966 the first US-market roadgoing GT 40 left for the States, to where most of the cars would be sent – only five stayed in Great Britain, while France, Germany, Switzerland and Italy each received one example. The Swiss car was finished by coachbuilder Hermann Graber, who gave it electric windows and some chrome ornamentation.

From 1 January 1967 production became the responsibility of JW Engineering, set up by John Wyer, former competitions director for Aston Martin, and John Willment. Manufacture of the GT 40 continued until June 1969, just after the second consecutive GT 40 win at Le Mans – both times with chassis 1075.

In the mid-1960s Ford had the temerity, with its GT 40, to take on Europe's most legendary makes – and not just on the race-track.

▲ *This GT 40 (P/1048) was acquired by the Brescia Corse team in May 1966; it later emigrated to France and in the early 1980s was restored in Switzerland by Franco Sbarro.*

◀ *Michael Martin's GT 40 (P/1082), built by JW Automotive in April 1969, is here on the Rallye de l'Ouest in 1971.*

FORD GT 40
1966 • 1969

▲ One of the seven GT 40 Mark IIIs has been on display for many years in the National Motor Museum at Beaulieu.

TECHNICAL SPECIFICATION (GT 40 MK III)

CONFIGURATION	MID-ENGINE; RWD
STRUCTURE	MONOCOQUE
BODY MATERIAL	GLASS-FIBRE
ENGINE	V8 (90 DEG)
VALVEGEAR	SINGLE CENTRAL CAMSHAFT
CAPACITY	4,736CC (95.5MM X 72.9MM)
POWER	306BHP AT 6,000RPM
FUEL SYSTEM	SINGLE FOUR-CHOKE HOLLEY CARBURETTOR
GEARBOX	5-SPEED ZF
WHEELBASE & TRACK	242.1CM; 140CM FRONT AND REAR
LENGTH/WIDTH/HEIGHT	429.3CM/177.8CM/104.1CM
WEIGHT	1,061KG
TYRES	FRONT 5.50 X 15IN; REAR 7.00 X 15IN
CHECK	
MAXIMUM SPEED	162MPH (260KPH)

SUMMARY OF OVERALL PRODUCTION OF THE FORD GT 40

THE RACING GT 40 MK I

- 5 prototypes (4.2-litre then 4.7-litre) in 1964 (GT/101 to 105).
- 6 prototypes (4.7) in 1965 (GT/1000 to 1005).
- 4 roadsters (4.7) in 1965 (GT/108, 109, 111, 112).
- 29 production cars, 1965–67 (GT40PR/1006 to 1010, 1014, 1017 to 1027, 1029, 1030, 1035 to 1042, 1048, 1073).
- 2 lightweight Alan Mann models in 1966 (AMGT-1 and AMGT-2).
- 11 production cars at JW in 1968–69 (GT40P/1074 to 1084) plus 7 incomplete chassis from 1970 to 1972 (P/1108 to 1114).
- 3 Mirages built at JW in 1967 (M.10001 to 10003).

THE ROADGOING GT 40 MK I

- 31 examples in 1966 and 1967 (GT40P/1013, 1028, 1033, 1034, 1043 to 1045, 1049 to 1072).
- 7 Mk IIIs from 1967 to 1969 (M3/1101 to 1107).

THE 7-LITRE PROTOTYPES

- 2 Mk II prototypes in 1965 (GT/106 and 107).
- 1 'X1' roadster in 1965 (GT/110)
- 8 Mk II-A prototypes in 1966 (GT40P/1011, 1012, 1015, 1016, 1031, 1032, 1046, 1047).
- 3 Mk II-A prototypes built by Alan Mann in 1966 (XGT-1 to XGT-3).
- 5 Mk II-B prototypes converted from Mk II-As in 1967 (GT40P/1015, 1016, 1031, 1046, 1047).
- 2 J-Car prototypes in 1966 (J-1 and J-2).
- 6 Mark IV prototypes in 1967 (J-3 to J-8).
- 2 Can-Am G7-A open cars in 1967 (J-9 and J-10).

THE ULTRA-RARE MARK III

In 1967 Ford created an even more exclusive and even more civilised roadgoing GT 40. It was called the Mark III and was unveiled at the April 1967 New York Motor Show. Ground clearance was improved, the power output further tamed, to 306bhp, and the suspension softened, while the monocoque was modified to allow better habitability, with a proper luggage boot in the tail. Finally, the looks were altered by the fitment of twin round lights and of small overriders in the front air intake.

▲ *The first Mark III built (M3/1101) is kept by the Ford Motor Company for promotion purposes.*

THE SEVEN GT 40 MK IIIs

1. GT40 M3/1101
DELIVERY: *April 1967*
REGISTRATION: *2B 510 (Michigan)*
BODYWORK: *Lhd prototype; dark metallic blue with black upholstery*
FIRST OWNER: *Ford Motor Company*
HISTORY: *New York Show, 1967*

2. GT40 M3/1102
DELIVERY: *December 1966*
REGISTRATION: *SPP 604D (GB)*
BODYWORK: *Blue with black upholstery*
FIRST OWNER: *JW Automotive (GB)*
HISTORY: *National Motor Museum, Beaulieu*

3. GT40 M3/1103
DELIVERY: *April 1969*
REGISTRATION: *MAX 777*
BODYWORK: *Purple with black upholstery*
FIRST OWNER: *Max Aitken*

4. GT40 M3/1104
DELIVERY: *October 1968*
REGISTRATION: *GT40-M3 (Florida)*
BODYWORK: *Dark green with black upholstery*
FIRST OWNER: *Joseph Candler (Florida)*

5. GT40 M3/1105
DELIVERY: *July 1968*
REGISTRATION: *NDF 2M*
BODYWORK: *Ice blue with black upholstery*
FIRST OWNER: *Herbert von Karajan*
HISTORY: *Sold at Barratt-Jackson auction, Arizona, 2003*

6. GT40 M3/1106
DELIVERY: *September 1968*
BODYWORK: *Ice blue with black upholstery*
FIRST OWNER: *Ford Motor Company (Dearborn)*

7. GT40 M3/1107
DELIVERY: *June 1969*
REGISTRATION: *DWC 8G (GB)*
BODYWORK: *Silver-grey with black upholstery*
FIRST OWNER: *Ford UK*
HISTORY: *London Motor Show, 1971*

1967 ▪ 1969

ALFA ROMEO 33 STRADALE

Racing in style

Alfa Romeo unveiled the prototype Tipo 33 in March 1967. It was an open racing barchetta built around an H-shaped tubular chassis and powered by an all-new mid-mounted V8. After having asserted itself in the GT class with the Giulia TZ and in the touring-car class with the Giulia GTA, Alfa Romeo made its ambitions clear in another arena. With this 2-litre prototype it was going to lock horns with Ferrari, then fielding its Dino 206S, and above all with Porsche and its 910s.

Alfa Romeo discreetly launched the Stradale – or 'street' – version of the 33 at the September 1967 Milan Racing Car Show, a few days before its formal announcement at the Frankfurt show. The body, gorgeously voluptuous, was the work of Franco Scaglione, who had been at Bertone for many years but had now gone freelance. Muscular, aggressive and sensual, the 33 Stradale was magnificently sculpted.

Six months after its appearance at Frankfurt the 33 Stradale was shown at the 1968 Geneva *salon* in a slightly modified form. There was now only a single lamp in each cowl, and air vents had been incorporated in the front wings after the first on-road test-sessions; some cars also had winding windows.

▶ *Between the first cars of September 1967 (right) and the example shown at the 1968 Geneva* salon *(below), the front-end styling evolved.*

TECHNICAL SPECIFICATION

CONFIGURATION	MID-ENGINE; RWD
STRUCTURE	MONOCOQUE
BODY MATERIAL	COMPOSITES
ENGINE	V8 (90 DEG)
VALVEGEAR	QUAD OVERHEAD CAM
CAPACITY	1,995CC (78MM X 52.2MM)
POWER	230BHP AT 8,800RPM
FUEL SYSTEM	SPICA FUEL INJECTION
GEARBOX	6-SPEED
WHEELBASE & TRACK	235CM; 135CM/144.5CM
LENGTH/WIDTH/HEIGHT	397CM/171CM/99CM
WEIGHT	700KG
TYRES	5.25M X 15 FRONT; 6.00L X 15 REAR
MAXIMUM SPEED	162MPH (260KPH)
NUMBER BUILT	18

THE '33' MARKED ALFA ROMEO'S RETURN TO ENDURANCE RACING. BUT THE THOROUGHBRED ALSO ATTRACTED NUMEROUS STYLISTS, NOT LEAST FRANCO SCAGLIONE, WHO PUT HIS SIGNATURE TO A SERIES OF TRULY INSPIRED BERLINETTAS.

▲ *In-house stylist at Bertone in the 1950s, France Scaglione had clearly lost none of his talent when it came to drawing up the Alfa Romeo 33 Stradale.*

Production of the 33 Stradale was taken on by the Autodelta workshops, run by Carlo Chiti. The body was built by Carrozzeria Marazzi at Caronno Pertusella, near Milan. In all, 18 examples of the 33 Stradale were built. Several cars had special coachwork:

- The Carabo, by Bertone, one of Marcello Gandini's masterpieces (Paris, 1968)
- The Roadster GS, by Pininfarina (Turin, 1968)
- The Prototipo Speciale, again by Pininfarina, and taking up the same body style as the Ferrari P5 (Paris, 1969)
- The Iguana, by Ital Design (Turin, 1969)
- The Spyder Prototipo Speciale, by Pininfarina (Brussels, 1971)
- The Navajo, by Bertone (Geneva, 1976)

McLAREN M6 GT

Broken dream

In 1969 the World Constructors' Championship was fought between Group 6 cars ('sports-prototypes', limited to 3,000cc) and Group 4 cars ('sports cars', with an upper limit of 5,000cc). If the latter enjoyed a substantial advantage in terms of engine capacity, in compensation they had to be 'production' cars, with a minimum of 25 examples made.

Four manufacturers set out to meet these criteria: Ford, whose GT 40 had been in regular production since 1966; Lola, which extrapolated the T70 GT from a model it had created for the Can-Am Championship; Porsche, who in the greatest of secrecy had made a series of 917s, these being completed in March 1969; and finally Ferrari, which was to enter its 512S in 1970. McLaren had the intention of joining this quartet by offering a closed GT based on an existing model.

As was the case with Lola, McLaren had an open sports car running in Can-Am. Indeed, its M6A had won the series in 1967 before being offered to private teams for 1968, as the M6B. The M6 GT which was derived from this was unveiled at the January 1969 Racing Car Show in London. Engineer Gordon Coppuck had developed a machine which was based on the structure of the M6A/M6B, but at the time of the show only a mock-up existed – the first car was still being built at McLaren's Croydon works, just outside London. The magnificent body was by Specialised Mouldings, to a design by Jim Clark (no – not that one…). Already, though, there was the question of how to manage to build 25 examples – it being the Trojan factory that would be given the task, following an October 1964 agreement between Bruce McLaren and the Lambretta-Trojan group.

It was then that someone had the idea of 'interpreting' the rules. Given that 28 examples of the M6B, the 'customer' version of the M6A, had been built, why not exploit this fact? It was thought that in order to obtain the precious certificate of homologation it would be sufficient, rather than making 25 new vehicles, merely to make the necessary bits to transform the M6B so it could be used in endurance events. The building of a batch of windscreens, doors and luggage boots was thus set in train, and an M6B with all these add-ons was duly presented

▶ *This M6 GT was for a long while the personal transport of Bruce McLaren.*

LONG BEFORE THE BIRTH OF THE MEDIA-BELOVED McLAREN F1, BRUCE McLAREN HIMSELF HAD NURTURED THE DREAM OF A GRAND-TOURING ROAD CAR.

McLAREN M6 GT
1969 • 1970

◀ *The David Prophet car was the only M6 GT which was regularly used on the track.*

TECHNICAL SPECIFICATION

CONFIGURATION	MID-ENGINE; RWD
STRUCTURE	MONOCOQUE
BODY MATERIAL	COMPOSITES
ENGINE	V8
VALVEGEAR	OHV; 2 VALVES PER CYLINDER
CAPACITY	4,990CC (102.1MM X 76.2MM)
POWER	430BHP
FUEL SYSTEM	4 TWIN-CHOKE WEBER CARBS
GEARBOX	HEWLAND LG500 5-SPEED
WHEELBASE & TRACK	245.1CM; 135.8CM/136CM
LENGTH/WIDTH/HEIGHT	411.4CM/185.4CM/101.6CM
WEIGHT	800KG
TYRES	FRONT 10X15; REAR 15X15
MAXIMUM SPEED	200MPH (320KPH)

to the FIA. But the federation wasn't fooled. Faced with this subterfuge, the M6 GT didn't receive its homolgation.

Accordingly Bruce McLaren gave up on the development of the M6 GT for competition and decided to steer the project towards a road car. Just one car took to the track, the example that Trojan had built in 1969 for David Prophet. He used it at Crystal Palace, as well as at Magny-Cours and Cognac in France. Bruce McLaren, meanwhile, used his own beautiful bright-red example to assess the viability of the project. Alas, the New Zealander's death in a testing accident on 2 June 1970 put an end to this tantalising dream. Beyond these two cars, and a third example delivered a little afterwards, a fair number of replicas have been built, but they are not recognised by McLaren as being authentic.

◀ *Top: An M6B being transformed into a 'sports' model, with doors and windscreen, at the Trojan factory in January 1969. Bottom: Beside the M6B, the first M6 GT was being readied.*

THE THREE McLAREN M6 GTs

1. BMR6GT-1
DELIVERY: *January 1970*
REGISTRATION: *OBH 500H*
BODYWORK: *Red; retractable headlamps*
FIRST OWNER: *Bruce McLaren*
HISTORY: *On show at the Museum of Transportation and Technology, Auckland, NZ*
LAST KNOWN OWNER: *Steve Dymand (US)*

2. M6B/50-001
DELIVERY: *March 1969*
BODYWORK: *Dark green; two round headlamps; converted into open car*
FIRST OWNER: *David Prophet*
LAST KNOWN SITUATION: *In Canada*

3. M6B/50-002
DELIVERY: *Unknown*
REGISTRATION: *M6BGT (California)*
BODYWORK: *Red; four cowled headlamps*
FIRST OWNER: *Trojan, then Ted Peterson (CA)*
HISTORY: Motor, *November 1975*
LAST KNOWN SITUATION: *California*

1969 • 1973

LOLA T70 Mk III GTR

Retirement in Switzerland

In the mid-sixties Eric Broadley, boss of Lola Cars Ltd, switched his attention to North America, abandoning the manufacture of sports-prototypes. It was only in 1967 that Lola returned to the fray, with the announcement of the T70 Mk III GT. It wasn't a totally new vehicle, being an extrapolation of the T70, a closed version of the sports-racer created in 1965 for the Can-Am Championship.

Two variants were announced at the January 1967 Racing Car Show in London: a 'works' version in Team Surtees colours and with an Aston Martin engine, and a version for privateers with a Traco-tuned Chevrolet V8 engine. Painted in British Racing Green, the T70 Mk III GT looked superb; it was the work of a certain Jim Clark, who worked for body experts Specialised Mouldings.

On the track, things were less stunning, and the first year's results were not exactly brilliant. The Lola-Aston failed at every fence, and only the Lola-Chevrolet saved the T70's honour with a fourth place in the 1967 Spa 1000km race. The next year was barely more encouraging. The Aston engine was put back on the shelf, while the privately-entered Lolas hardly shone, despite the respectable number that were to be found on grids.

At the 1969 Racing Car Show, Lola displayed a developed version of the T70 Mk III GT, the Mk III-B GT. Its main distinguishing points concerned the bodywork. The doors now opened conventionally, instead of gullwing-fashion, and the bonnet incorporated twin headlamps and took on more angular but aerodynamically more efficient lines. Meanwhile, the roadholding and braking were improved and a perceptible reduction in weight was achieved. Thus modernised, the T70 achieved its first – and only – great international success in the 1969 Daytona 24-Hours. It has to be said that the magnificent blue machine

▲ *The Lola T70 Mk III GTR as it appeared at the 1969 Racing Car Show.*

TECHNICAL SPECIFICATION

CONFIGURATION	MID-ENGINE; RWD
STRUCTURE	MONOCOQUE
BODY MATERIAL	COMPOSITES
ENGINE	V8 (90 DEG)
VALVEGEAR	OHV; 2 VALVES PER CYLINDER
CAPACITY	4,990CC (102.1MM X 76.2MM)
POWER	430BHP AT 6,200RPM
FUEL SYSTEM	4 TWIN-CHOKE WEBER CARBS OR LUCAS FUEL INJECTION
GEARBOX	HEWLAND 5-SPEED
WHEELBASE & TRACK	241.3CM; 144.8CM/146.1CM
LENGTH/WIDTH/HEIGHT	420CM/185CM/101CM
WEIGHT	860KG
TYRES	FRONT 5.50 X 15; REAR 7.00 X 15
MAXIMUM SPEED	200MPH (320KPH)
NUMBER MADE	28 (14 MKIII GT AND 14 MK III-B GT), PLUS 11 MADE BY SBARRO
CHASSIS NUMBERS	MK III GT: BETWEEN SL73/101 AND 135 MK III-B GT: BETWEEN SL76 138 AND 151

In the great era of sports-car racing, Lola had a walk-on part in the war being waged between Porsche, Ferrari and Ford. It was only a small step from there to dream of selling a prestige roadgoing T70 . . .

in the Sunoco colours benefited from meticulous preparation by Roger Penske.

At the same Racing Car Show another T70 attracted attention: the Mk III GTR (chassis SL73/135). This was a road-going example prepared for Lola by Franco Sbarro in Switzerland, leather upholstery, walnut veneer wood trim and air-conditioning transforming the interior. The car was sent to the US for evaluation by Carl Haas, but Lola soon decided not to proceed with the project.

When manufacture of the T70 ended, and Lola moved from Slough to Huntingdon, the wily Franco Sbarro recovered the T70's tooling. In this way eleven new 'Sbarro Type Lola' cars were born on the shores of Lake Neuchatel between 1971 and 1975, with the cars being called Sloughi from 1973, in homage to their home town. Once again, the savvy coachbuilder had done himself proud. Some of his Lolas were as comfortable and sophisticated as a limousine, having a leather interior, a television, telephone and stereo. The choice of engine was at the customer's discretion, with Franco Sbarro outlining various possibilities: a Ford or Chevrolet V8… or perhaps a Ferrari V12. Everything was possible with the magician of Yverdon.

▲ *A Sloughi made by Franco Sbarro in the 1970s.*

◀ *The Lola T70 with Aston Martin power, as campaigned in 1967.*

1971 ■ 1974 LANCIA STRATOS HF

Rallying's first supercar

The history of the world rally championship turned a new page with the coming of the Lancia Stratos HF. Until then all the car-makers participating in the championship had used – and promoted – mass-production vehicles, chosen from their range on the basis of their potential to be uprated as appropriate. With the Stratos, Lancia took a radically different approach: this time it turned its back on everything in its current range, and started with a clean sheet of paper. Conceived from the outset as a competition machine, with no thought of a hypothetical 'civilian' rôle, the Stratos was created in conjunction with Bertone and stylist Marcello Gandini. The car was sculpted for the road: squat, balanced, compact in the extreme, it was perfect for threading together the bends of the Col de Turini or the Inzecca Pass. The wheelbase was ultra-short, for the best handling, and the view to the front was totally panoramic, as the drivers had wanted. Playing on in-house synergies, Lancia raided the corporate parts-bins of the Fiat group for the power unit, Ferrari providing an engine derived from the V6 of the Dino 246 GT, but adapted for mounting transversely.

The Stratos was unveiled at the 1971 Turin show, in a white livery, and for its configuration if nothing else drew on the radical wedge-shaped Stratos concept car shown at Turin the year before. The Stratos HF project was supervised by Cesare Fiorio, Lancia's competitions and commercial director, with engineer Gianpaolo Dallara looking after development. When Dallara left for Williams in 1973, to look after the Iso Formula 1 car, English former racing driver Mike Parkes replaced him.

The Stratos was to be seen again at the 1972 Turin show, this time in a striking satin-finish bright red; this was a prelude to production beginning at Bertone at the beginning of 1973, with the key aim of obtaining Group 4 homologation. This was duly gained in October 1974, but there arose some doubt as to how many Stratos had really been made. It was certainly the case that Lancia had a lot of difficulty finding homes for these no-compromise devices, which were too brutal for just any old driver, and too inconvenient for daily use.

But in compensation, in the World Rally Championship the Stratos excelled. Even before it had been homologated it had its debut on the 1972 Tour de Corse, driven by Sandro Munari – but the serious business began two years later. For three consecutive seasons, from 1974 until 1976, Lancia was World Rally Champion, notching up eleven outright victories thanks to the Stratos. Then the

▶ *Marcello Gandini's masterpiece for Bertone, the Stratos HF revolutionised the history of rallying.*

▶ *Corsica was one of the Lancia Stratos HF's favourite hunting grounds...*

With the arrival of the Stratos, the rally world entered a new era, Lancia being the first to create a car tailor-made for winning the championship.

commercial strategy of the Fiat group changed: the board back in Turin preferred to push the Fiat 131 Abarth, which was more relevant to their everyday products. But the Stratos continued to shine in World Championship rallying, in the colours of various private teams, winning the Monte Carlo in 1977 and 1979 and the Tour de Corse in 1979 and 1981.

TECHNICAL SPECIFICATION

CONFIGURATION	MID-ENGINE; RWD
STRUCTURE	MONOCOQUE
BODY MATERIAL	COMPOSITES
ENGINE	V6 (90 DEG)
VALVEGEAR	QUAD OVERHEAD CAM
CAPACITY	2,418CC (92.5MM X 60MM)
POWER	190BHP AT 7,400RPM
FUEL SYSTEM	3 WEBER TWIN-CHOKE 40 IDF
GEARBOX	5-SPEED
WHEELBASE & TRACK	218CM; 143.3CM/145.7CM
LENGTH/WIDTH/HEIGHT	371/175CM/111.4CM
WEIGHT	980KG
TYRES	205/70 VR 14
MAXIMUM SPEED	143MPH (230KPH)
NUMBER BUILT	498
CHASSIS NUMBERS	829ARO 1001TO 1008; THEN 1509 TO 1992

1978 ▪ 1981

BMW M1

Noble pretext

Aware that its heavy and bulky 6-series coupés had limited development potential, BMW decided to undertake the design of a true competition car. The only snag was that to obtain Group 4 (GT class) homologation, regulations demanded a minimum production of 400 cars.

Founded in 1972, BMW Motorsport GmbH, the sporting division of BMW, was entrusted with Project E26, which would ultimately lead to the M1. In its broad lines the M1 was born out of the BMW Turbo, the concept car French stylist Paul Bracq had created in 1972; but this time the styling was the work of Giorgio Giugiaro at Ital Design, although the link with the Bracq design was clear.

As the M1 was always going to be marginal in terms of its industrial viability, BMW envisaged the car being manufactured by Lamborghini, and from May 1977 the Sant'Agata Bolognese company was involved with testing of the prototype. But Lamborghini soon found itself in financial difficulties, to the point that in April 1978 BMW annulled the contract. In the end it was Ital Design who built the M1, at Montcalieri, near Turin, final assembly being assured by Stuttgart coachbuilder Baur.

The M1 has to be regarded as a road car derived from a competition car, and not the other way round. In many respects the M1 borrowed from race-car technology, not least in the chassis design with its wishbone suspension: all that was done was to replace the Rose joints with more comfortable rubber bushing.

Beyond the restraints of homologation the intention was indeed to develop a road car that could happily be used on a daily basis. It is because of this that the M88 engine was so docile, just as was the sweet-changing gearbox.

The exterior style, bearing the unmistakeable imprint of Giugiaro, had a fine balance, but the interior was frankly austere, recalling the car's original vocation of being more sporting than touring. That said, the ergonomics were satisfactory, access was easy despite the low-slung body, and the cloth-and-leather seats gave perfect support. The only niggle was a total lack of interior stowage, the only storage space being in the boot behind the engine.

In the end the BMW M1 had a disappointing career both commercially and in

AT THE BEGINNING OF THE 1980S BMW, WANTING TO MOVE UP A GEAR IN MOTOR SPORT, DECIDED TO MAKE A GT COUPÉ DESIGNED SPECIFICALLY FOR RACING.

the sporting field. Production, at 453 cars, barely exceeded the 400 units required, and competition successes were limited to a few podium positions. The most spectacular showing was at 1979's Le Mans, with the Poulain/Winkelhock/Mignot car – but the spectacle was less that the BMW finished sixth but that it had a fantasy paint-job by no less an artist than Andy Warhol…

◀ ▲ *With the passing of time the simple and pure Giugiaro lines have come into their own; they were inspired by those of Paul Bracq's BMW Turbo.*

TECHNICAL SPECIFICATION

CONFIGURATION	MID-ENGINE; RWD
STRUCTURE	TUBULAR FRAME
BODY MATERIAL	COMPOSITES
ENGINE	6-CYLINDER IN-LINE
VALVEGEAR	TWIN OVERHEAD CAM; 24V
CAPACITY	3,453CC (93.4MM X 84MM)
POWER	277BHP AT 6,500RPM
FUEL SYSTEM	BOSCH MECHANICAL INJECTION
GEARBOX	5-SPEED ZF
WHEELBASE & TRACK	256CM; 155CM/157.6CM
LENGTH/WIDTH/HEIGHT	436/183.4CM/114CM
WEIGHT	1,300KG
TYRES	205/55 VR 16 FRONT; 225/50 VR 16 REAR
MAXIMUM SPEED	162MPH (262KPH)
NUMBER BUILT	453

1982 ■ 1983

LANCIA RALLY

Apotheosis of a saga

One was within one's rights to believe that the career of the Lancia Monte-Carlo had ended at the closure of the 1981 season, with a second world-Championship title in silhouette-formula racing. It was certainly true that up to that point the Monte-Carlo had suffered a chaotic existence. In the beginning it was supposed to have carried a Fiat badge, because it was effectively a development of the little mid-engined X1/9 roadster. Then it underwent its first competition development at Abarth, running in the 1974 Giro d'Italia under the Abarth 030 name. Finally it emerged in 'civilian' guise at the 1975 Geneva Motor Show, as the Lancia Beta Monte-Carlo. This car with its hazily mapped-out destiny had a less than glorious commercial career, with only 7,695 examples made between 1975 and 1981.

It was thanks to new openings in the world of motor sport that it was to come back from the dead. The arrival of a new set of rules in 1979 at last provided an opportunity to propel the Beta Monte-Carlo onto centre stage: the World Sports Car Championship was opened to Group 5 cars (of roughly 2-litre capacity), called the 'silhouette' class on account of their obligatory superficial resemblance to production cars.

After Lancia's success in this arena, there was a new leap forward in 1982 when the company announced its return to the rally scene with a new evolution of the Monte-Carlo. The project bore the number 037 in Abarth's numbering system, Abarth by this time being the sporting arm of the Fiat group. A first prototype was developed by Gianpaolo Dallara, manufacture of the production vehicles then being entrusted to Pininfarina, who had created the original body style. Relative to the Beta Monte-Carlo the wheelbase was extended by 5½in (14cm) and the shell was widened to take 16in wheels, while there were various aerodynamic addenda. The engine, still Fiat-derived, was boosted by a volumetric supercharger. The Lancia Rally was announced at the April 1982 Turin Motor Show, having already received its Group B rally homologation. For the 1983 season the valiant Italian carried off the title, despite the dogged opposition offered by the Audi Quattro. This made it the last winner of the World Rally Championship to have only two-wheel drive. It thus closed the book on a chapter in the history of rallying.

▶ *Using the base of the Lancia Monte-Carlo it had originally designed, Pininfarina was responsible for producing the Rally.*

TECHNICAL SPECIFICATION

CONFIGURATION	MID-ENGINE; RWD
STRUCTURE	TUBULAR FRAME
BODY MATERIAL	COMPOSITES
ENGINE	4-CYLINDER IN-LINE
VALVEGEAR	TWIN OVERHEAD CAM; 4 VALVES/CYL
CAPACITY	1,995CC (84MM X 90MM)
POWER	205BHP AT 7,000RPM
FUEL SYSTEM	WEBER TWIN-CHOKE 40 DCNVH; ROOTS-TYPE SUPERCHARGER
GEARBOX	5-SPEED ZF
WHEELBASE & TRACK	244CM; 150.8CM/149CM
LENGTH/WIDTH/HEIGHT	391.5/185CM/124.5CM
WEIGHT	1,170KG
TYRES	205/55 VR 16 FRONT; 225/50 VR 16 REAR
MAXIMUM SPEED	137MPH (220KPH)
NUMBER BUILT	257
CHASSIS NUMBERS	001001 TO 001217 001301 TO 001320 (EVOLUTION 1) 001401 TO 001420 (EVOLUTION 2)

Born to contest the World Rally Championship, the Rally was a superb way of brilliantly closing the book on the career of the Beta Monte-Carlo, a car which hardly had a good start in life.

1984 • 1986

FORD RS 200

The anachronism

In the 1980s numerous manufacturers took part in the World Rally Championship with vehicles homologated in Class B. These hybrid cars all had one thing in common: they were real prototypes, with their own configuration and with sophisticated mechanicals wrapped in a familiar silhouette. The Peugeot 205 Turbo 16, Citroën BX 4TC, MG Metro 6R4, Audi Quattro Sport and Lancia Delta S4 were all of this breed. These confections had to be made in a minimum quantity of 200 cars, a number of vehicles that was not easy for the market to absorb, as the cars were expensive, impractical and not particularly attractive. All except one: the Ford RS 200.

Stuart Turner was the instigator of the RS 200 project for Ford Motorsport, a company outpost situated at Boreham in Essex. Ford chose to counter existing Group B contenders by creating a radically different product, one that had no link with any existing saloon. The idea was to design a dedicated rally car, as Lancia had done with the Stratos and as Ford had itself already tried with the stillborn GT70. Tony Southgate, a big name in Formula 1 (at BRM and Shadow, most notably), was engaged to work on the chassis. In September 1983 construction of a first prototype was begun, and the car was officially unveiled at the 1984 Turin Motor Show. The body, which was certainly attractive enough, was the work of Ghia, whose styling department was then the responsibility of Filippo Sapino.

The car's competition debut was in the September 1985 Lindisfarne Rally. In January 1986 Ford was in a position where it could show the Fédération Internationale du Sport Automobile (FISA) the 200 examples required by the homologation rules: Reliant had looked after assembly, while Tickford had trimmed the cars.

Then in the midst of the 1986 season came the bombshell, when FISA banned Group B cars from the World Championship with effect from the following year. The first rallies of the year had been marred by several fatal accidents which called into question the excessive performance of these specialist machines. Group B was accordingly abandoned, in favour of Group A cars that were presumed to be less powerful and thus not capable of the same speeds. In these circumstances the RS 200 didn't have the time to prove its mettle. This was a shame, as on its first championship outing, the 1986 Swedish Rally, it came home a promising third.

Of the 200 cars built, only a hundred were sold, with great difficulty, the last in 1988. The remaining cars were kept by the factory, either being used in competition or being dismantled to provide a stock of spare parts.

The RS 200 was a well balanced car, thanks to its evenly-split front/rear weight distribution. The body was hardly breathtakingly efficient aerodynamically (the Cd was 0.42), on account of the various add-ons. Despite the Tickford connection – and the Ghia badge that road cars carried – the RS 200 was never regarded as a car of noble extraction.

IN THE HEADY DAYS OF GROUP B RALLYING, FORD STOOD OUT FROM ITS RIVALS BY CONTESTING THE WORLD RALLY CHAMPIONSHIP IN A CAR THAT HAD A REAL SENSE OF STYLE.

TECHNICAL SPECIFICATION

CONFIGURATION	MID-ENGINE; 4WD
STRUCTURE	TUBULAR FRAME WITH CENTRAL BACKBONE
BODY MATERIAL	COMPOSITES
ENGINE	4-CYLINDER IN-LINE
VALVEGEAR	TWIN OVERHEAD CAM; 16V
CAPACITY	1,804CC (88MM X 77.6MM)
POWER	250BHP AT 6,800RPM
FUEL SYSTEM	ELECTRONIC INJECTION; GARRETT TURBOCHARGER
GEARBOX	5-SPEED
WHEELBASE & TRACK	235CM; 150.2CM/149.8CM
LENGTH/WIDTH/HEIGHT	400CM/176.4CM/132.2CM
WEIGHT	1,250KG
TYRES	225/50 VR 16
MAXIMUM SPEED	143MPH (230KPH)
NUMBER BUILT	200 (OF WHICH 24 'EVOLUTION')

▲ *The RS as shown by Ghia in November 1984.*

◀ *The RS 200 hardly had the chance to prove itself in competition.*

McLAREN F1

Armed with six wins in the Formula 1 Constructors' Championship (1974, 1984, 1985, 1988, 1989, 1990), McLaren launched into the manufacture of a formidable road car following the setting up of McLaren Cars Ltd in 1989. Shown at an avant-première in Monaco in May 1992 as a mock-up, the first running McLaren F1 was finished at the end of that year. With its composites monocoque, the McLaren drew on the most avant-garde technology available. The requirements of technical director Gordon Murray majored on ergonomics, visibility, aerodynamics and compact overall dimensions. In the first instance the F1 stood apart from its contemporaries in the arrangement of the cockpit, with the driving position being central, flanked either side by a passenger seat. Before taking delivery, the owner had a fitting session to optimise seat and pedal positioning.

Over and above its functionalism, typified by the unflamboyant but ergonomically correct instrumentation, the McLaren had all necessary comforts, such as air-conditioning and electric windows, while the interior was trimmed in leather and Alcantara. The bespoke Kenwood audio system in particular gave a superb performance, thanks to its 12 speakers: Gordon Murray was after all a hardened music-lover…

The charismatic engineer had succeeded in creating a vehicle that was lighter than all its competitors. Despite its long wheelbase, the McLaren was also astonishingly compact. For the engine, Gordon Murray teamed up with his old friend Paul Rosche at BMW, with whom he had worked in his days at Brabham. The aerodynamics were especially studied, with careful attention given to underbody airflow, and to such important details as the pop-up rear spoiler that contributed to braking balance, and the fan that increased the inherent downforce of the underside design. All the aerodynamic features were perfectly integrated into the shape, designer Peter Stevens, who had previously worked for Lotus and TWR, coming up with a harmonious form that stylishly married aesthetics with high technology.

Manufacture of the F1 continued until 1998, but in the meantime the McLaren distinguished itself in competition in the guise of the F1 GTR, most notably winning

▶ *The McLaren F1 was unveiled in May 1992 in the form of this mock-up.*

For its designers, the McLaren F1 had to be capable, without major modification, of going from road to track, as a result of an alliance of refined comfort and hard-and-fast driving ability.

McLAREN F1 1992 • 1998

▲ *One of the original features of the F1 was its central driving position.*

TECHNICAL SPECIFICATION

CONFIGURATION	MID-ENGINE; RWD
STRUCTURE	CARBON-FIBRE MONOCOQUE
BODY MATERIAL	COMPOSITES
ENGINE	V12 (60 DEG)
VALVEGEAR	QUAD OVERHEAD CAM; 48V
CAPACITY	6,064CC (86MM X 87MM)
POWER	627BHP AT 7,400RPM
FUEL SYSTEM	ELECTRONIC ENGINE MANAGEMENT
GEARBOX	6-SPEED
WHEELBASE & TRACK	271.8CM; 156.8CM/147.2CM
LENGTH/WIDTH/HEIGHT	428.8CM/182CM/114CM
WEIGHT	1,080KG
TYRES	235/45 ZR 17 FRONT; 315/45 ZR 17 REAR
MAXIMUM SPEED	230MPH (370KPH)
NUMBER BUILT	69 (PLUS 6 F1 LM, 28 F1 GTR AND 3 F1 GT)
CHASSIS NUMBERS	PROTOTYPES: XP1 TO ZP5 ROAD CARS: 001 TO 018, 020 TO 025, 028, 029, 031, 033, 036 TO 040, 042 TO 053, 055, 057, 060 TO 075. F1 LM: XPLM, LM1 TO LM5 F1 GTR: 01R TO 028R F1 GT: 56XPGT, 054GT, 058GT

at Le Mans in 1995. The car essentially differed from the road-going model only in its rear spoiler. For its third racing season, in 1997, the F1 GTR was more radically modified, being given a lengthened body. The creation of the 911 GT1 by Porsche had obliged Gordon Murray to react, and distance the race car from its road-going sister, something he had wanted to avoid.

There were 69 normal-spec road cars made, plus six F1 LMs, with the same aerodynamic add-ons as the GTR, and three F1 GTs, with a long tail in the style of the 1997 GTR. Beyond this, between 1995 and 1997 the factory produced 28 F1 GTRs, of which nine had the long-tail body.

▲ *The GTR version was essentially distinguished from the normal F1 by its additional aerodynamic equipment.*

▶ *The F1 LM combined the F1's regular mechanicals with the exterior detailing of the GTR.*

1994 • 1996

VENTURI 400 GT

Escape route

Born in 1986, the Venturi project had difficulty getting through the subsequent recession, despite the acknowledged quality of its products. The arrival of a more sporting variant and the creation of a racing championship specifically for Venturi cars allowed the marque to bounce back. Logically enough called the Trophy, the car designed for the championship was announced in February 1992 at the Centre Internationale de l'Automobile, in Paris. At the same time Venturi unveiled an F1 single-seater powered by a Lamborghini engine. Clearly there was no limit to the firm's ambitions…

The technical development of the Trophy was undertaken by Claude Poiraud, who with Gérard Godefroy had been behind the creation of the Venturi. When Poiraud left in April 1992, development work became the province of Jérôme Kieffer. For four years the Venturi Trophy kept the Gentlemen Drivers Trophy rolling, and kept the marque's name in the public eye. In June 1994, in the middle of the third season, Venturi's new boss, Hubert O'Neill, unveiled the 400 GT. This was quite simply a road-going version of the Trophy, retaining that car's dramatic silhouette, evolved by Gérard Godefroy from his original 1980s design. The 400 GT differed only in such changes as were necessary for daily use: increased ground clearance, pop-up headlamps, an engine cover no longer integrated with the rear bumper, and a more plush cockpit with air-conditioning, electric windows and door mirrors, leather trim, and carbon-fibre decoration. The most notable technical feature of the 400 GT was its carbon-fibre brakes (both discs and pads), which were a 'first' on a road car. Developed by Carbone Industrie, they made an appreciable improvement to unsprung weight; they also lasted longer and could resist temperatures of over 1,000 degrees. The engine was derived from

▶ *Type-approved for road use, the Venturi 400 was directly derived from the Venturi Trophy (inset) created for the Gentlemen Drivers Trophy.*

TECHNICAL SPECIFICATION	
CONFIGURATION	MID-ENGINE; RWD
STRUCTURE	BACKBONE CHASSIS
BODY MATERIAL	COMPOSITES
ENGINE	V6 (90 DEG)
VALVEGEAR	SINGLE OVERHEAD CAM PER BANK; 24V
CAPACITY	2,975CC (93MM X 73MM)
POWER	408BHP AT 6,000RPM
FUEL SYSTEM	ELECTRONIC ENGINE MANAGEMENT; TWIN TURBOCHARGERS
GEARBOX	5-SPEED
WHEELBASE & TRACK	250CM; 157CM/168CM
LENGTH/WIDTH/HEIGHT	414/199CM/117CM
WEIGHT	1,150KG
TYRES	245/40 ZR 18 FRONT; 295/35 ZR 18 REAR
MAXIMUM SPEED	180MPH (290KPH)
NUMBER BUILT	13 (PLUS 10 TROPHY MODELS CONVERTED FOR ROAD USE)

THE VENTURI COMPANY RECEIVED A BOOST THANKS TO THE CREATION OF THE GENTLEMAN DRIVERS TROPHY, WHOSE STAR TURN WOULD GIVE BIRTH TO A HIGHLY EXCLUSIVE GT COUPÉ.

the Alpine A610's modest V6, but was up-gunned by EIA, an engine specialist that had already collaborated with Venturi on several projects.

The Gentlemen Drivers Trophy ran from 1992 to 1995. In parallel Venturi boosted its sporting programme with a spectacular participation in the Le Mans 24-Hours: seven 500 LMs were entered in 1993. Then the following year Jürgen Barth, Patrick Peter and Stéphane Ratel came together to create the BPR championship, in order to bring a bit of life to the moribund world of endurance racing. Venturi became an active participant, with three victories in 1994 – at Dijon, Montlhéry and Spa. It was felt there was cause for optimism, but reality soon chimed in, as so often is the case, and the following season was a catastrophe as much in sporting as in commercial terms.

The company was put in liquidation in 1996. A Thai group temporarily took charge, but it was only with the providential arrival of Gildo Pastore in 2002 that Venturi was revived.

1997 – 1998

PORSCHE 911 GT1

A monster for the road

Since 1963 Porsche's destiny had basically been built around the 911. Evolved in a seemingly infinite number of variants, and as capable of winning on the sandy tracks of the Paris-Dakar as on the snowy roads of the Monte Carlo Rally, the 911 also dished up a memorable victory in 1998's Le Mans with the 911 GT1. Before this, the monster spawned a few roadgoing examples to tempt a handful of enlightened enthusiasts…

A year passed between the first Le Mans appearance of the GT1, in 1996, and the unveiling of the road-car proposal in April 1997. For this variant the familiar Porsche cabin ambience was retained, but access was compromised by the width of the side skirts, the low build of the car, and the presence of a tubular reinforcement to bar entry. Once at the wheel, you discovered an astonishingly docile machine. Relative to the race car, the engine, linked to a monodisc clutch, had lost a little puff, but the power remained phenomenal. The carbon-fibre brake discs, meanwhile, had given way to steel items that were more forgiving in everyday use.

The silhouette was breathtaking. If certain stylistic details of the regular 911 were evident, the roadgoing GT1 nevertheless displayed the same caricatural lines as the racing model, in particular the flattened glasshouse and the aerodynamic addenda that gave such phenomenal downforce. At the rear a bulky spoiler wrapped around the car's rump, itself topped by a strut-mounted aerofoil. The front stayed relatively sober, but the sides were swollen out around the doors, with extended wing panels encompassing huge vents behind the front wheels and smaller inlet vents in the rear wings. Certain demanding customers, however, requested a more stylistically refined body. To please them, the air vents, treated without compromise on the racers, were integrated into the shell with a little more attention to aesthetics, most notably with a sweeping moulding extending the wheelarch line into the doors.

Contrary to the countless homologation-special series – 911R, Carrera RS and RSR, 934, 935, 911 SC/RS, 911 GT2 and GT3 – the 911 GT1 only hit the street after its debut on the race-track.

▲ *A 'civilised' 911 GT1, as sold at the Bonhams auction in Monaco, in May 2003.*

▶ *The 911 GT1 in its warpaint, for the 1997 racing season.*

Porsche has always relied on its customers to add to its competition laurels – and even the most extravagant extrapolation of the 911 has been adapted for road use.

TECHNICAL SPECIFICATION

CONFIGURATION	MID-ENGINE; RWD
STRUCTURE	TUBULAR FRAME
BODY MATERIAL	CARBON-FIBRE
ENGINE	6-CYLINDER HORIZONTALLY-OPPOSED
VALVEGEAR	TWIN OVERHEAD CAMS PER BANK; 24V
CAPACITY	3,164CC (95MM X 74.4MM)
POWER	544BHP AT 7,000RPM
FUEL SYSTEM	ELECTRONIC ENGINE MANAGEMENT
GEARBOX	6-SPEED
WHEELBASE & TRACK	250CM; 150.2CM/156.8CM
LENGTH/WIDTH/HEIGHT	471CM/195CM/117CM
WEIGHT	1,075KG
TYRES	285/35 ZR 18 FRONT; 335/30 ZR 18 REAR
MAXIMUM SPEED	193MPH (310KPH)
NUMBER BUILT	30

MERCEDES-BENZ CLK-GTR

A time for opportunism

Propelled forward by Helmut Werner, Mercedes-Benz had an extraordinary last decade of the 20th century. In the sporting field it led from the front in Formula 1 and in endurance racing. At that time the governing bodies of the sport wielded bad faith with a masterliness such as only they could command. Ever since the invention of endurance racing, symbolised by the 1923 creation of the Le Mans 24-Hour race, regulations have frequently been based on the specious argument that competition benefited the car of the man in the street. Armed with this logic, the body shapes of countless production cars have been superimposed on pure competition mechanicals.

In the context of the FIA-GT championship, manufacturers were asked to field machines capable of generating road versions. Toyota, Nissan, Panoz and others rushed into the breach: they were entitled to run an out-and-out prototype so long as they showed a 'civilian' version, road-registered, even if there were no plans for production.

The Mercedes-Benz CLK-GTR was one of the rare machines genuinely to be put into production. Between December 1998 and July 1999 the Stuttgart firm sold 22 examples of a road-going version of its endurance champ – keeping back three cars for its private collection. Manufacture was looked after at Affalterbach by AMG, which Mercedes-Benz ended up acquiring on 1 January 1999. The cars thus wore the identity 'Mercedes-AMG'.

At first glance the road CLK-GTR looked very much like the competition version: it could mainly be distinguished by the better-integrated spoiler on the rear deck,

▶ *With the CLK-GTR, Mercedes-Benz achieved what had not been possible with the 300 SLR in the 1950s: to put on the road a real racing prototype.*

The CLK-GTR dominated the 1997 and 1998 seasons of the FIA-GT championship, and then gave birth to a small run of road cars built by Mercedes subsidiary AMG.

MERCEDES-BENZ CLK - GTR 1998 • 1999

▶ *Better integration of the aerodynamic addenda was the main concession made for the production model, relative to the racing CLK-GTRs.*

▲ *The CLK-GTR failed at Le Mans but won the FIA-GT championship in 1997 and 1998.*

TECHNICAL SPECIFICATION

CONFIGURATION	MID-ENGINE; RWD
STRUCTURE	TUBULAR FRAME
BODY MATERIAL	CARBON-FIBRE
ENGINE	V12 (60 DEG)
VALVEGEAR	QUAD OVERHEAD CAM; 48V
CAPACITY	6,898CC (89MM X 92.4MM)
POWER	612BHP AT 6,800RPM
FUEL SYSTEM	ELECTRONIC ENGINE MANAGEMENT
GEARBOX	6-SPEED SEQUENTIAL
WHEELBASE & TRACK	267CM; 166.5CM/159.4CM
LENGTH/WIDTH/HEIGHT	485.5CM/195CM/116.4CM
WEIGHT	1,545KG
TYRES	295/50 ZR 18 FRONT; 345/35 ZR 18 REAR
MAXIMUM SPEED	199MPH (320KPH)
NUMBER BUILT	25

by the big air scoops on the sides of the front air-dam, and the deeper wheelarch returns necessitated by the smaller tyres. The carbon-fibre body weighed only 87kg, and included front and side impact beams designed to absorb energy in an accident. The engine was derived from the V12 of the SL 600, but with a larger capacity. At the same time the unit lost 30-odd kilos thanks to the use of precious metals: there were titanium big-ends, forged pistons, and a lightened flywheel. The valvegear was also revised, with bigger valves and reprofiled camshafts, and there was dry-sump lubrication.

In the cockpit everything was trimmed in leather or suede, set off by carbon-fibre inserts. But when the machinery was given its head the thrust in the driver's back was so impressive that one was soon reminded of the CLK-GTR's motor-sport origins. It was certainly a long way from the meek-and-mild production CLK of which the glasshouse was supposedly evoked by the GTR's shape…

CLK-GTR

SALEEN S7

The GT spirit

The motor car has a formidable capacity for adaptation. In the course of its first century of existence it has overcome all the crises, all the economic recessions, all the challenges thrown at it, because it has always been able to respond to whatever were the new facts on the ground. After the disappearance of the 'supercar', condemned by the economic crisis of the early 1990s, it was difficult to imagine that new manufacturers would take a bet on such a marginal market, and one so vulnerable to economic volatility. And yet in the last years of the century a handful of new marques has emerged: Victor Müller revived the Dutch name Spyker, for example, while in Italy argentinian Hector Pagani launched the Pagani Zonda.

In the US, Steve Saleen came into the public eye at the same time, positioning himself in the upper reaches of the automotive industry by creating a car of real originality. When he unveiled his S7 at the August 2000 historic races at Laguna Seca, in Monterey, California, Saleen was no unknown in the world of motor sport: since 1984 he had been race-preparing Ford Mustangs and selling these in small quantities.

With the S7, Saleen moved to another level. The car was no longer an adaptation of a mass-produced model, but was a completely fresh design with contemporary mid-engined architecture. Equally impressive, only 18 months passed between the first sketches and the first customer car.

From the outset the S7 had been conceived to be suitable both for road use and for competition. The structure was based on a tubular chassis reinforced by a composites honeycomb, developed – along with the wishbone suspension – in conjunction with English specialist Ray Mallock Ltd. Power, meanwhile, came from a dry-sumped V8 created by Bill Tally around an aluminium Ford block. These carefully evolved mechanicals were then wrapped in an aggressive but beautiful body designed by Phil Frank.

▶ *Saleen had succeeded in creating a small specialist firm in the shadow of the big American combines.*

At the dawn of the 21st century a new name made its appearance in the supercar world: Saleen. Once again, the very spirit of 'Grand Tourism' was made flesh.

SALEEN S7
2000 • 2004

The Saleen S7 had its racing debut during the 2001 season. It participated in particular in the US Championship and at Le Mans, but had to confront better-armed homegrown rivals such as the Chevrolet Corvette and the Chrysler Viper GTS-R.

Saleen has kept his promises. Born for the track, the S7 is made in a road version. The hand-building of the cars takes place in Irvine, on the outskirts of Los Angeles, with final assembly of vehicles for Europe and Middle East being looked after by Saleen's British affiliate.

Total production is set not to exceed 300 – 400 examples, in the course of the intended five-year production run. Just enough to maintain the thoroughbred bloodline…

▲ *The Saleen S7 locks horns on the track with the Chrysler Viper and the Chevrolet Corvette.*

▶ *The sleek lines of the Saleen are the work of Phil Frank.*

TECHNICAL SPECIFICATION	
CONFIGURATION	MID-ENGINE; RWD
STRUCTURE	TUBULAR FRAME WITH HONYCOMB REINFORCEMENT
BODY MATERIAL	CARBON-FIBRE
ENGINE	V8
VALVEGEAR	SINGLE CENTRAL CAMSHAFT; 2 VALVES PER CYLINDER
CAPACITY	7,011CC (104.8MM X 101.8MM)
POWER	550BHP AT 6,400RPM
FUEL SYSTEM	ELECTRONIC ENGINE MANAGEMENT
GEARBOX	6-SPEED
WHEELBASE & TRACK	270CM; 174.8CM/171CM
LENGTH/WIDTH/HEIGHT	477.5CM/199CM/104CM
WEIGHT	1,246KG
TYRES	275/30 ZR 19 FRONT; 355/25 ZR 19 REAR
MAXIMUM SPEED	199MPH (320KPH)
NUMBER BUILT	STILL IN PRODUCTION

HomeLink
5
Automationdirect.com
BOSCH
Cutler-Hammer
ROAD&TRACK

Contents

Photographs all from the personal collection of Serge Bellu.